D0770148

THE ALCHEMY OF POSSIBILITY

Reinventing Your Personal Mythology

by

CAROLYN MARY KLEEFELD

Foreword by Laura Archera Huxley

Contact Information:
Published by Merrill-West Publishing, P.O. Box 1227, Carmel, CA 93921
Phone (831) 644-9096. Fax (831) 644-9097 e-mail: info@voyagertarot.com
Website for Merrill-West Publishing: http://www.voyagertarot.com

Fine Art Cards and information on the author's art available from
Atoms Mirror Atoms, Inc., P.O. Box 221693, Carmel, CA 93922.
Phone / Fax (831) 626-2924
Website for Atoms Mirror Atoms: http://elfi.com/illuminati.html

Library of Congress Number: 98-66079

ISBN 1-886708-03-7

First Edition
All excerpts from the Tarot, unless otherwise noted, are from *The Tarot Handbook*, by Hajo Banzhaf, translated from German into English by Christine M. Grimm, reproduced by permission of U.S. Games Systems, Inc., Stamford, CT 06902 USA. Copyright © 1993 by U.S. Games Systems, Inc. Further reproduction is prohibited.

All excerpts from the I Ching, unless otherwise noted, are from *The I Ching or Book of Changes*, the Richard Wilhelm Translation, rendered into English by Cary F. Baynes, with a Foreword by Carl G. Jung. Copyright © renewed 1977 by Princeton University Press. Reprinted by permission of Princeton University Press.

In most chapters of *The Alchemy of Possibility*, the entire card or hexagram from which a quote is derived applies, and therefore its title is highlighted. In instances where the quote alone applies but not necessarily the entire card or hexagram, the location of the quote is merely noted in brackets.

Book and Cover Design: Irene Morris / Morris Design, Monterey, CA
Photograph of the Author: ©1998 Dennis Wyszynski

Cover Image: Detail from *"Favorite Flower of Apollo,"* by the author.
Back Cover: *"Zen Face,"* by the author.

TO *the* GODPARENTS *of*
THE ALCHEMY *of* POSSIBILITY

John Larson (Wolf), whose loving ears played back the strings of my heart.
These songs were recorded and blossomed my garden sprouting the love that
birthed *The Alchemy of Possibility*

Kirtana, wild dove, whose patient angel-heart and organizational genius,
edited and cultivated the essential seeds from my journals
(written between 1989 and 1997) for the birth of *The Alchemy of Possibility*

Patricia Karahan Holt, whose vast generosity of being and deep-rooted connection
to my work made possible and orchestrated the final birthing of
The Alchemy of Possibility

Mytheos Holt, whose ancient soul and nine-year-old self poetically slept on the
couch between Patricia and me as we edited many a night into the night

David Wayne Dunn, who held the light of *The Alchemy of Possibility* in his heart
throughout its many transformations

Francis Jeffrey, cyber-muse and catalyst of the interactive marriage of The I Ching
and Tarot as an organizational form for this book

With loving appreciation to:
Laura Archera Huxley and David Jay Brown

With gratitude and love to:
Julie King, Merrill-West Publishing

Special thanks to:
Deborah Johansen, Irene Morris and Dennis Wyszynski

***The Alchemy of Possibility* was also metabolized by:**
Ann West, Dr. Carl Faber, Edmund Kara, Dr. Oscar Janiger, Dr. Timothy Leary,
Nina Graboi, Ram Dass, Terence McKenna, Dr. John Lilly, Ralph Abraham,
Rupert Sheldrake, Nick Herbert, Candace Pert, Lorena Del Campo, Carla Kleefeld,
Claudia Kleefeld, Barry and Louise Taper, Marilyn Bihari, Alice Russell, Gina Russell,
Ronna Emmons, Lucy Christopher, Kay Walters, Marion and Alan Hunt-Badiner,
Barbara Draper, Michelle Ryan, Gail Bengard, Max Flandorfer, Sharyn Adams,
Naomi Kern, Attila Kocs, Evan Landy, Linda Jacobson,
Katya Williamson, David Steinberg, Evelyne Blau, William Melamed,
Toni and Valentine Burton and the unmentioned.

The Alchemy of Possibility could not have manifested as a book without my parents:
"Pops" Mark Taper, my celestial guide and most benevolent patron, and
Amelia Taper, who passed on to me her artistic heritage and, together with "Pops,"
the shining inspiration of their humanitarian ethics.
The Gemini publication of this book commemorates
my mother's birthday.

CONTENTS

Section 1:
Cultivating a higher perspective

Section 2:
Understanding physical reality and the laws of nature

Section 3:
Personal
challenges

Section 4:
Relating to
ourselves, others,
family, society,
earth, the cosmos

FOREWORD

Reading *The Alchemy of Possibility* brought back a specific memory of Aldous: Three days before he died he was speaking with extraordinary vitality, in spite of his heart-breaking weakness, about a "new kind of literature, different from what anybody has ever written." "How different?" I asked. Aldous, with a wonderfully happy expression in his voice, unexpectedly like his strong, vital self answered: *"By bringing it all in!"* *

I have the impression that in *The Alchemy of Possibility*, Carolyn Mary Kleefeld also aspires *to bring it all in*. And indeed she has brought many dimensions into this book of prose, poetry and painting. She has brought the abundance of her talent and the intensity of her passion. The result is a journal that reaches many levels of being — hers, ours and our world's.

Kleefeld touches on psychological, spiritual, ecological and physiological topics. One is her cry for liberation. To attain it, "all it requires," she says, "is either faith or exhaustion." In that statement, she presents the spiritual and psychological parts of herself — but then, the impartial observer adds, "and usually both."

Like all nature-mystics, Carolyn has a symbiotic relationship with nature. *The Alchemy of Possibility* might remind us, not through statistics but through poetic prose, that the Golden Rule is to be applied to every tree, every rock, every creature and every thing on the planet. The poem *is you, is me* says it all.

There is a numinous presence in her identification with nature. Often in Kleefeld's artwork there is a mingling of contrasting feelings: The painting, *Must Flee the City*, has a mocking quality and, at the same time, evokes compassion for the bewildered, lonely woman attempting to escape the crushing lunacy of the city.

In writing freely about her amorous, spiritual and mundane life, Kleefeld offers, I believe unintentionally, a sort of effective intangible therapy for "surfing the waves of existence."

Each chapter of *The Alchemy of Possibility* connects a theme from *The I Ching*, and from Tarot Commentaries, with writing and painting by the author, presenting a challenging, interwoven tapestry spanning across centuries and spaces.

The Alchemy of Possibility is to be kept nearby and enjoyed slowly, and if you have a question in mind, open it at random, and you might — just might — find *an* answer. There is no promise of finding *the* answer. In fact, Kleefeld writes, "The answer is to be so still that the questions stop"— a charming way to put the reader on the spot.

One of the most touching and enlightening passages in the book describes Carolyn's dynamic relationship with her father, a modern real-world tycoon, who had a grandiose and successfully realized materialistic vision. Both daughter and father are visionaries and have been estranged for years by their divergent visions. The daughter, victim and beneficiary of her father's accomplishment, is now strong and independent. She goes to her ailing father and finds the old giant — who, through his enterprises has once fed thousands of people — now so weak as not to be able to feed himself. With intelligent dedication and through scrupulous research, the daughter finds and uses the best medical and psychological means to assist her father through that all-important transformative period before and into death. All past conflicts vanish — father and daughter, at one time two roaring rivers in a warring country, now softly melt into that quiet sea of compassion always open to all who ask.

— Laura Archera Huxley
Los Angeles, California,
August, 1997

*A full account of this conversation is related on pages 205-208 of *This Timeless Moment:*

A Personal View of Aldous Huxley, by Laura Huxley. (New York: Farrar, Straus & Giroux, 1968)

INTRODUCTION

The Alchemy of Possibility, like life itself, will be many things to many people. A book of spiritual revelations and psychological insights to some, an inspiring odyssey of the imagination to others, *The Alchemy of Possibility* documents the archetypal sojourn of the visionary artist. It also serves as a how-to book; a navigation manual for the alchemical transformation of consciousness, providing instructions for assembling an "architecture" of the higher spheres — what Carolyn Kleefeld has termed the "Sixth Dimension." As with her previous poetry collections, Carolyn bares the escalating evolution of her soul, and speaks out with a bold and admirably honest voice on such spiritually essential topics as love, immortality, reality, the discovery of one's deeper nature and the search for higher meaning. Like Anaïs Nin, Carolyn bravely explores inner dimensions that are at once both intimately personal and archetypically universal, delicately woven together with sensuous passion; and as with Kahlil Gibran, we witness the philosophical fruits of one who has undergone profound spiritual lessons.

Following the tradition of William Blake and Herman Hesse, *The Alchemy of Possibility* is a poetic blend of mysticism and imagination. In harmony with the visible rainbow and the musical scale, *The Alchemy of Possibility* follows the law of octaves, recapitulating the evolutionary journey from the earth to the heavens. As with the literary works of James Joyce, there are many levels of meaning woven into *The Alchemy of Possibility*. It was deeply inspired by the six-thousand-year-old Chinese *The I Ching*, one of humanity's oldest surviving mystical texts; since then, a contemporary translation of this timeless message has long been overdue.

Each chapter can be viewed like a ray of sunlight through a crystal prism, where a full spectrum of meaning is encoded in a multileveled series of layers. One gleans from each passage the message that one is "ready" to hear, in coincidence with the synchronicity of the moment.

A series of extraordinary paintings and drawings capturing various aspects of the ecstatic vision accompany and complement the text. These mythic expressions of the Jungian collective unconscious, and cyberdelic DNA mindscapes of paradise, can be viewed as windows into supernatural worlds, or as a kind of inter-dimensional Tarot sequence. They illustrate the transitions in *The Alchemy of Possibility* and provide us with a peek behind the scenes of existence, wherein many secrets of nature are revealed. In your hands you hold a treasure chest overflowing with "rippling revelations" and "postcards from heaven," which you can keep near your bed and consult, like a trusty companion, again and again. Carolyn's words and visions will surely serve as an empowering inspiration for many generations to come.

— David Jay Brown
Ben Lomond, California,
April, 1997

LETTER TO THE READER

I think of *The Alchemy of Possibility* as a way of looking at the elements that compose the occasion of possibility. And I am receptive to the possibility inherent in every moment. *The Alchemy of Possibility* implies that it is always possible to view life from a broader perspective, to metabolize change rather than resist it, and to be ourselves alchemized in the process. This process is an endless one of surfing and navigating the waves of existence, emerging out of the formless in ever-moving form. Throughout these transformations, this shedding of skins, our vital essence continues as the core of our experience.

The metamorphic aspect of our being, evolving in the endless seasons of mortal and eternal life, I have named the I Change. As us, she is the heroine of our odyssey. I envision this *being* as a vapor-like entity concocted from a mysterious recipe of all that has ever been and will be.

Ultimately we are all Eye, all seeing in the shifting light of consciousness. Our inner light sees beyond the range of our outer sight. It is with our inner sight that we seed our outer blossom. When our perceptions change, we see things differently. And when we see things differently, we evolve.

When I read *The Alchemy of Possibility*, it seems like a long hypnotic poem sung to myself, the mythology of a Taoist-Pantheist creating an aesthetic and philosophical dimension amidst the opaque density of our frantic times. Often while writing this book I have felt like a bird collecting materials for its nest. I fly about spinning threads of philosophic thought for the Sixth Dimension, my inner home. Art is love in creation, and love is an art created. In the purity of the unconditioned, the seed may thrive.

I find that to know the hearts of other artists greatly intensifies the inspiration of their art. In this spirit I offer these writings, paintings and reflections. My DNA, my strange and unique code of being is spilling into letters that record my peculiarity and uniqueness of experience. As I attempt to express the usually invisible climes, transitions of my inner climates, I hope you will be relieved to have another be so open, so human, so pathetic and potentially inspiring. This is an artist's translation of change, a record of refining one's granules on the shores of time.

I realize that life, its transitions, its manifestations are usually so gradual that it is only in contrast to another cycle that we recognize change or progress. I think of sand slowly, gradually breaking down from a cliff at the beach and how many centuries it took to make that movement possible. How long for the boulders, rocks to become granules of sand. How long for the alchemy of earth, air and seas to come into that one space in infinity's time.

So when I see change as gradual, I'm aware that life's movement is composed of a relentless accumulation of additions and subtractions, gains and losses, positive and negative existences, each of which, even in its absence, adds to the expanding universe of consciousness "by the presence of its absence," (Hue Neng, AD 600).

A realization or revelation may have had countless previous births. With this in mind, I yield again to the eternity of time's faceless clock, before our minds give it hands or digits.

Nature is our most advanced technology. And because the vital essence within each of us is intrinsic to Nature's perpetuity, we can be confident of our inherent power. With this in mind, I encourage each of us to live fully our alchemy of possibility. Let us spin our most evolved integration, our new mythology into the Cosmic Loom, transforming the opaque into the transparent.

— Carolyn Mary Kleefeld
October, 1997

The Alchemy of Possibility offers an inner-active meditation in which the deeper psyche of the reader-participant is revealed, propelling the discovery of his or her own way.

SUGGESTIONS

FOR EXPLORING

THE ALCHEMY OF

POSSIBILITY

The Alchemy of Possibility gives reader-participants a meditative film in which to develop themselves. This uncontrived, interactive type of self-discovery is possible because it comes from the life process itself rather than from someone taking authority and projecting his or her own structure on another. Mirroring the dynamic symbolism of systems such as the Tarot and *The I Ching*, this book can serve as an oracle or advisor of the wider potentials inherent in every question or situation. It can be turned to consciously or in meditation when we seek guidance, reorientation or fresh insights.

One of Carolyn Mary Kleefeld's paintings or drawings is thematically paired with each chapter. Readers may gaze at the images until one of them ignites a particular interest. Drawing on the marriage of visual and written language, the reader can then peruse the corresponding text.

Alternately, readers can glance through the list of chapter titles in the front of the book, or the images and poems listed in the back, until a particular title resonates. The corresponding chapter can then be read. Or one can hold a question in mind, open the book intuitively and let the synchronicity of the moment guide the way. Also the book can be read through in its entirety.

The Alchemy of Possibility is arranged into four general sections of fourteen chapters each. These sections are analogous to the four suits of the Tarot's Minor Arcana, which through time evolved into the four suits of our common playing cards. Each section delineates a certain focus, clarifying the terrain of possibilities for reinventing our own mythologies. The categories are as follows:

1. The qualities and attributes we need to develop and cultivate in order to create or change our personal mythology;

2. The underlying laws of manifest reality we must understand in order to participate consciously in this process;

3. The personal challenges the evolving soul must face and transform along the path;

4. The reflection and progress that relationship provides in the quest, beginning with the relationship to oneself and extending outward to lovers, friends and families; to our society and the Earth; to the heart of the Cosmos.

The Alchemy of Possibility offers an inner-active meditation in which the deeper psyche of the reader-participant is revealed, propelling the discovery of his or her own way.

"Favorite Flower of Apollo"

"It is only through a living personality that the words of the book ever come fully to life and then exert their influence upon the world."

"The Great Treatise"
from The I Ching,
Wilhelm/Baynes translation

"Zen Face"

CHAPTER 1

THE ZEN

MOMENT

THE
I CHING:
[FROM 5. HSÜ /
WAITING
(NOURISHMENT)]
*We should not worry and
seek to shape the future
by interfering in things
before the time is ripe....
Fate comes when it will,
and thus we are ready.*

The way of the lover is to be fully present. May we live the potential of the moment, shedding the distractions of the mind's busy plans. No direct experience of the wondrous is possible without being emptied of distraction.

I release my attachment to outcomes, to living the future of myself in the present. By releasing outworn patterns, the gestures of the past, we live amidst the winds of change, embracing the unfamiliar. The past is but a dried leaf, returning to the soil to begin again. How brief our candle's flame; waste not its wick.

Time is a localized concept, good for appointments, while Nature's pulse resounds in the endless seasons, cycles of the continuum. As the poet Robinson Jeffers observed, "There are times when one forgets for a moment that life's value is life; any further accomplishment is of very little importance, comparatively."

We can not force anything essential; our rushing is a sign of anxiety, a lack of cosmic perspective. Substance requires the gradual layering of the seminal.

We are traveling through the endless molecular moment in which every atom of living existence is a part. In this vaster melody that my song has rejoined, I hear all of time resound in the present. I receive messages spontaneously, without thought, where treasure is always found — in the present moment, beyond our fabrications, beyond mental plans.

We are traveling through the endless molecular moment in which every atom of living existence is a part.

Microcosm*: Resting in Infinity

Today is a seamless, lyrical day. No distractions come into my sanctuary via people or answering machine. The flights of thoughts, images drift by on an unfolding reel of memories. I find them unappealing as they attempt to seduce me, take me away from my root experience.

I am discovering anew the beauty of simplicity, of enjoying what is so easy to have, yet so elusive. I know this vast, yet simple world of universe is available if I am. I rest in the hinterland of the divine, with a handful of keys to nowhere.

* see glossary

the seasonal instant

The endless blue heavens
reflect paradise
in the shimmering steam
of a timeless summer day

The tide's echoes
vibrate the beginning
in every wavering leaf
and random pebble

The hum of orchestration,
the tidal winds of change
move to ever distant futures
in the seasons of an instant

"A Numen Gazes"

CHAPTER 2

BEING STILLNESS AND OPENING TO RECEIVE

THE I CHING:
52. KEN / KEEPING STILL, MOUNTAIN

True quiet means keeping still when the time has come to keep still, and going forward when the time has come to go forward.... When a man has thus become calm... he has that true peace of mind which is needed for understanding the great laws of the universe and for acting in harmony with them.

TAROT:
IX THE HERMIT
We find repose and, above all, are separate from bustling activity and crowds of people.... On the level of consciousness this card means that we withdraw in order to come closer to ourselves, free and uninfluenced by the opinions of others.

When I am amidst confusion and ambivalence, I remember to yield, living the music of just *being*. I disengage from the movies of the mind, the romantic tragedies, the cops and robbers, the entertainments of the ego. My drives relax into a more powerful skeleton, moving with ease to a unique and unfamiliar rhythm. In this wondrous experiment of living the miracle of the unclasped, life happens. I let the great gardens flourish in their ripening of golden fruits.

The flowering of invention, of our sensibilities, requires a primarily safe environment, the luxury of time and space. I let the seeds of rising consciousness be dormant long enough to germinate. In this regenerating stillness, meadows within bud again; the imagery of my seeds appears as paintings, drawings, writings. I become the unpainted canvas, the blank page of the paper.

In being stillness, instinct calmly guides; decisions come of their own accord. The balance of my holographic mandala is restored.

The answer is to be so quiet that the questions stop.

From a relaxed state of being, the seminal gestates. Without anxiety or defense, we are in tune with the resonant knowledge, the platonic wisdoms that murmur from the earliest pools.

The answer is to be so quiet that the questions stop. From the lake of silence, answers resound as echoes from the primal text. We hear the *lost language of unheard sound,* the Eternal Symphony that carries us to the pure state of *a priori.* All becomes known in this intimacy of dialogue. We evolve into the Sixth Dimension*, the realm of holographic consciousness.

* see glossary

being silence

in commemoration of Aldous Huxley

Being silence
The lucid lake
An empyrean expanse
A highly organized weaving
Is silence
Woven intricately within

In being silence
Each transmitting thread
Virtuous unto itself
Is a vital stream
In tantric connection
Within the vast design

"The Tree Face of Metamorphosis"

CHAPTER 3

EMBRACING

CHANGE

The I Change* asks for the faith, the courage to live constantly in the unfamiliar, to ride the waves beyond self-ego, as in my painting, *Riding the Quantum Wave*. Self is a localized illusion. We are temporal representatives of a universal principle. Our "core" is our essential nature: the unconditioned in dialogue with the ever-constant.

When we fear the unfamiliar, growth is stunted. Let us surf the realities, ride the wave's crest. Although sometimes we may be dashed upon the rocks of life experience, the jolts may offer abrasion for refinement. The challenge is to be resilient in our response to life's demands. All it requires is either faith or exhaustion and usually both.

Each of us is a beam of light offered to our days. The more receptive, the more acute our sensibilities, the greater the possibility for new experience, re-vision, bridges toward further systems of comprehension. Without the receptive, there is no creative. With each symbiotic breath, possibility transforms our present atomic existence into yet another creation. Our unique rhythm resonates in the Eternal Waltz.

THE I CHING:
3. CHUN /
DIFFICULTY AT
THE BEGINNING

The situation points to teeming, chaotic profusion: thunder and rain fill the air. But the chaos clears up.... A thunderstorm brings release from tension, and all things breathe freely again.... in the chaos of difficulty at the beginning, order is already implicit.

TAROT:
6 OF SWORDS

The 6 of Swords...deals with our reaching new shores and having to leave old ones, without knowing what is really waiting for us on the other side. In this respect it shows the grief of parting, insecurities, fears, and worries, but also a certain curiosity and tension about what is to come.

* see glossary

May we live in a perpetual state of reinvention.

Karma can be an old record that plays autonomously in spite of us. When we disengage from the repetition of old records and stale sentimentality, we discard the preconceptions of who we are, yielding to transition.

We are living in the bottleneck of transition; change comes at the eleventh hour. As a new species, we will evolve into the Sixth Dimension.

Eternally, we are all the I Change. The conceptual doors of life and death do not exist. The atom is forever reforming, regardless of its visibility. Our immortality lies in our capacity to re-form. Metamorphosis is the elixir of life. May we live in a perpetual state of reinvention.

spring equinox

I lie here
in my ancient chambers
origins gleaming
through candle's wick,
flames of ancestors glow
through my being;
                I await...

What will the next clime be?
Which force will breathe my nostrils,
see through my eyes,
change me without asking?

I await in my small largeness;
an expansion inhales me
with a tingling pulse

                Life lives me
as its instrument refining
I watch the stormy skies
                for what next?

Feeling, as the tree outside,
stronger from the bending winds,
the spine more flexible,
the spirit more questioning
                following the child

"Domains of Grace"

Chapter 4

CHAPTER 4

DROPPING DESIRE —

THE ECSTASY OF

DETACHMENT

THE
I CHING:
27. I / THE CORNERS
OF THE MOUTH
(PROVIDING
NOURISHMENT)
*He who seeks nourishment
that does not nourish reels
from desire to gratification
and in gratification craves
desire.*

Wanting is itself a thief, taking from life with misperception what is already there. Without attachment we yield to expanding awareness, to the bounty of ourselves, the universe. To accept what *is* rather than struggle in a whirlpool of conflicting desires is to climb with grandeur the steps to one's throne in the imperial gardens within.

When we *want,* we lose our inner kingdoms; feeling incomplete, we give ourselves away to our symptomatology. If we live from our symptoms, trying to fill these needs, we produce extra work. Life can be more simple without such self-imposed chaos.

It has been difficult to take a deep breath — my inhale has been obstructed by the furniture of purpose. Desires have distorted my boundaries, extending me beyond myself. A return to simplicity relieves me of the fragmented complexity of our civilization.

> Wanting is itself a thief, taking from life with misperception what is already there.

Our poli-economic systems engender dependency, cripple us in ever-accelerating consumerism. We are brainwashed to desire, to buy. In our insatiable need for consumption and distraction, our appetites imbalance us, leading to self-destruction. If our desires take us out to hunt, perhaps we are the ones getting trapped.

As expectation is at its root, attachment is fraught with suffering. When fear blocks transition, needs are born. The warring human is an accumulation of conflict and pain. Healing may come from the realization that we already have everything we need to live on a higher spiritual level. Let us travel within; the treasure we seek awaits.

To evade desire, our own trap, let us re-learn detachment, "the ecstasy of indifference," to quote my friend, the sculptor Edmund Kara. We can use what we do not have to give us something else, to allow the unfamiliar to occur. From the germinating seed within comes the regenerative soul. How then can *want* exist?

Microcosm: Cobalt Tears of Release
With the guidance of sublime intuition, I shed the skins of outworn attachment. A few cobalt tears come with the cleansing, the letting go. The freedom from my clinging psyche becomes the wind for my sail. I can accept myself and others without seeking what we are not. I can let *be* what *is*. I can *not know*.

Now, when I feel the lament of longing, I understand that want is from some inward poverty, an inner disconnection or imbalance. If I stop thinking I need what *is not* and enjoy what *is*, the perception of lack vanishes of its own accord.

the winds of change

There's a green seed
in my eyes tonight
A mossy blanket
over my heart

In your night's mane
stars untumble
In my hand
a fresh current
moves my pen

Will tomorrow again
hold the core of yesterday?

Will the unknown face
of green seed,
that promise inherent
in life's germ
be able to grow?

Or will it abort
in disillusion's will?
Be but a toy
for the restless force

Only tomorrow's breath,
the liberation of detachment
will let the wildflowers grow

To then be plucked
by the winds of change,
the seed of life eternal

This wilderness of chance
asks one thing of me
To try not to see its face
nor name its life to be

But merely let it pulse
in the darkest night

To give it to the heavens,
the orbit of its choice

And I but a vehicle
for life's thirst

Only when out of touch
do I try to know,
to name its face

"The Witness of the More Sees with Golden Seeds"

CHAPTER 5

THE

OVERMIND

VIEW

Our Overmind must discriminate among the kaleidoscope of realities for us to author our book of life. As the camera of our lens, we may perceive ever-new vistas. Once our "observer" takes space shots from myriad vantage points, our interpretation can be made with an affectionate indifference. The expression and fulfillment of our inherent nature becomes more possible.

"A passion for distance," poet Benjamin DeCasseres says, "brings us constantly to the furthest edge of abstraction." To the explorer, abstraction is of primary interest. Let us integrate the Overview, discern with dispassionate compassion, ascending despite gravity, viewing our evanescent yet infinite selves.

It behooves us to keep the Witness of the More* as our personal guardian, sentinel or sheep dog. The Observer of our Theater of Illusion must ever be on duty. With the Witness of the More as Overmind, our personal *impersonality,* we become inscrutable spies, made incisive by detachment. In this neutrality of disengagement, we may see through the games of existence.

THE
I CHING:
35. CHIN / PROGRESS
The hexagram represents the sun rising over the earth. It is therefore the symbol of rapid, easy progress, which at the same time means ever widening expansion and clarity.... The higher the sun rises, the more it emerges from the dark mists, spreading the pristine purity of its rays over an ever widening area.

TAROT:
3 OF WANDS
The 3 of Wands...shows that we have reached the heights through a long arduous ascent and are now allowed to have a broad view of the luminescent horizon from a secure observation point.

* see glossary

The Observer of our Theater of Illusion must ever be on duty.

Cul-de-sacs, or "double-binds," as anthropologist Gregory Bateson termed them, require us to step out of futility, letting the Witness observe the mind's conditioned habits. The Witness of the More recognizes the recycling of our illusions, the denial and passivity that dulls us. The self-referencing Witness integrates our experience, weaving our learnings into a deeper comprehension. Integration is a constant process; we emerge seamless as an egg.

Let us be in alignment with our highest intention. To serve ourselves and thus humanity requires mastery over emotional plagues. With sensitivity, let us listen and observe our behaviors.

Microcosm: The Observer's Eye
When I am fatigued, my Onlooker temporarily vanishes. The Witness of the More disappears from my drawings. Even my eyes look opaque, like framed windows with no view. During such times I remind myself to let go of the need to react.

Yearning for silence, the black of night, the empty canvas, the empty page, I breathe deeply, discarding the ghosts that haunt. I invite detachment. When I am quiet enough, I can observe the myriad facets of my internal movie. Another layer of philosophic pigment reassures, protects. The symbiosis of Union relieves me from the trap of humanity's body. The poetic metabolism is ever expressing itself. How I welcome the quieter appetite, the Observer's Eye.

the inflammable witness

An inner burning
of leafless branches,
of parks with wood benches,
the smoldering of the green

Relief surfs
on a wave of indifference

New suns sprout
from scorched ground,
from the inert earth

As my Nature
re-alchemized, metabolized
now is the future

This incessant electrical burning
This breathing circulation of All
blazes through gardens
and deep cobalt seas

While the mind
outside of the aquarium
*   stands dry:*

The inflammable Witness
*   of the More*

"Astral Gardens"

CHAPTER 6

TENDING

THE INNER

GARDEN

THE
I CHING:
27. I / THE CORNERS
OF THE MOUTH
(PROVIDING
NOURISHMENT)
*If we wish to know what
anyone is like, we have
only to observe on whom
he bestows his care and
what sides of his own
nature he cultivates and
nourishes…. Mencius says
about this: "He who
cultivates the inferior parts
of his nature is an inferior
man. He who cultivates
the superior parts of his
nature is a superior man."*

In listening to our souls, we cultivate ourselves, the Earth. Without our inward soul-trodden path, our gardens are desert isles, isolated from the vast streams of other spirits, alien unto ourselves. Our flowers, fruit trees and plants remain barren without love, the fertilizer of infinity.

As the soul-heiress of my existence, I claim sovereignty to my kingdom, devoted to tending my gardens in paradise. Do my desires integrate with this dedication? I prune my garden with discrimination, learning what is essential for regeneration. I let the wind's gust and shimmering sunlight use me as their trellis, as a receptor and transmitter of the winds of change.

By living simply, we tend the wilderness of ourselves. If we keep our stepping stones clear of choking vines, psychic traps, our paths will reveal themselves and we may follow. The simple has within it the direct path to paradise. Through tending our inner garden, we liberate our souls.

In my garden I see that I echo Nature's innermost process, discarding dry leaves, rusty concepts — prejudices that, as dead brush, clutter my views. Although their function

Through tending our inner garden, we liberate our souls.

is past, old ties hold up a dead vine. In the same way, we hang onto what is no longer vital. After a drought many casualties appear on the battlefields of Earth. Dead roots and severed branches lie everywhere. As we also suffer in our times of spiritual drought, let us create a space for the birth that pollinates from death, a space for the re-arranging, re-positioning of Change's next form.

Rejoicing in my restoration, I continue to plant seeds in my marrow-soil, trusting the mystery that spores regeneration.

Microcosm: A Humble Tree

I feel a fragile budding of new and green health, of promise, of effervescent pulse. Ah, life regained reflects itself in direct simplicity. This is only possible with a nervous system untainted by the constant quirks of the interfering, conditioned mind.

My body-heart asks me to let go of all grievances and broken leaves, to return whole to the naked innocence of birth. I return as a humble tree to my nature. I yield to the Greater; I will tend my garden.

oh garden, how true you are

Oh garden, how true you are
How your grasses speak to me
How the color of your leaves beds me
Oh garden, how true you are

You ask for rain
You are so patient
With the endless drought

You'd like some flowers
To blossom your earth
Yet you wait and wait
The rains do not come

With cracked soil
And hardened heart
Oh garden, how true you are

I know from your earth-skin
The state of your health
I see no flowers blooming
The seeds have been eaten

I wait with you, my garden
My soul, my patience
For life's tender balm
To ease the burning urge
For love's moisture

"Adjusting the Perceptual Eye"

CHAPTER 7

EDITING, SIFTING, REFINING

As I walk my cosmic connection, I recognize the need to be a sieve, selecting and refining which ingredients may enter. By taking the time to refine my process, I am not just another leaf blown by the storm.

The sifting, editing of thoughts and attitudes into a more comprehensive integration must be constant. Let us recognize the cumbersome furniture of our minds, because without the capacity to discriminate, we become scattered, dispersed. Our Editorial Owl* is ever-vigilant, serving the Tao.

I re-read *Letters to a Young Poet* and yearn to be in my Rilkean being again, my most intimate. Experiences of the past weeks settle as strata of dust upon my earthly soul. Heavy fog dampens, nurtures and insulates. Flowers of new insight sprout. Scenarios are edited from the movie of my mind. I return to paganism, the simple, the unhurried, the poetic. I re-emerge, a strange slinking creature pulling its unrecognizable form from the seas of the unconscious.

THE I CHING:
57. SUN /
THE GENTLE
(THE PENETRATING, WIND)
In human life it is penetrating clarity of judgment that thwarts all dark hidden motives.

TAROT:
ACE OF SWORDS
The Ace of Swords represents the principle of higher reason, which as perceptive power leads to clarity, lucidity and resoluteness…the effect of the mind is shown here in its illuminating, clearing, and freeing manner. It is a matter of penetrating and analyzing a problem with all of the available acuteness, without losing the perspective of the whole….

* see glossary

After every tide
of ecstasy, suffering
and balancing,
I peer, a strange
and wet embryo,
into the mirror of
current reality.

~

After every tide of ecstasy, suffering and balancing, I peer, a strange and wet embryo, into the mirror of current reality. Who am I in relation to others, to the universe? Each time I emerge, my vision moves to a slightly more prismatic view, to further comprehension, if only in the futility of human conjecture.

If unedited material from self-produced movies clutters my life, I notice the recent challenges, their effect. Recording my subsequent understandings, I architect my philosophy, navigating with its guidance.

ingredients of the gods

Oh, the density
sensitivity must bear

Let us endeavor
to see through
those other forces

Recognizing they too
are God's ingredients

Stepping aside,
if need be

"Trees at Lunar Lake"

CHAPTER 8

THE
MIRRORED
LAKE

The White Voice murmurs from the lake of the uncluttered mind. Through our streams of pure water, we see the underpinnings of existence. From our clearest lake, eternity speaks. Books may validate these teachings, but only through direct experience may they be metabolized.

We are instruments ever to be perfected. When we are too busy, when our streams are unreceptive to the subtle sensings of inner current, our whirlpools grasp and consume. We are unable to feel our infinity, our expanded rhythm-voice. Let us keep our channels clear, our circulation in poetic resonance with our souls. Drop the static, mechanized mind. In seeing through the complexities, we refine; life becomes more transparent. Like the Hindu of timeless pasts with a passion for out-of-body travel, we may enter astral realms experiencing creation, its suspension, its void. *Things* require maintenance; the *Other* offers solace.

Let us be Voidoids* again, detach and become the undeveloped film, recognize the recycling of illusions as more dirty laundry to be bleached into oblivion.

***

THE I CHING: 35. CHIN / PROGRESS

The light of the sun as it rises over the earth is by nature clear. The higher the sun rises, the more it emerges from the dark mists, spreading the pristine purity of its rays over an ever widening area. The real nature of man is likewise originally good, but it becomes clouded by contact with earthly things and therefore needs purification before it can shine forth in its native clarity.

***

* see glossary

Like the Hindu of timeless pasts with a passion for out-of-body travel, we may enter astral realms experiencing creation, its suspension, its void.

As filmmakers, we use ourselves as cameras; the more clear and multifaceted our lens of perception, the more open we are to receiving the essential.

Microcosm: Quiet Pools

Ah, Nature is returning. I can hear the myriad birds. Their song vibrates, resounding within me. Today is the first day in two weeks I have been able to rest fully again in my nature, in the simple rhythms of existence. Free of mind-sobering and emotional gravities, I am regaining my capacity for receptivity. The static and discord of the human world, of my humanness, slowly moves out with the sea's currents. My pools settle into lakes where my reflections mirror the greater existence again.

in resoundance

Enshrouded
in the bible black night
the unknown inhales me
into its darkest womb
There, we are one pulse again

The extraneous
is put to rest
in the ancient caves
          of origin

Swimming in a metallic pond
of moon beams,
my song re-chords integration

Darkness develops my day's film
dissolving and re-forming

In the ebb and flow
of tidal rhythm
In resoundance
with the seas below

"Malibu Impromptu"

FANNING
OUR UNIQUE
FLAME

Each of us is a flame within the eternal kiln, casting an essential ray into infinity. As unique instruments, we each experience life differently. Our varied experiences are the tools that sculpt our lives.

The fragmentary effect of life's experiences shatters our souls upon the rocks as the storm's waves sculpt their passions onto the lone boulder. Our scriptures are inscribed by the quill of Nature's forces, our texts preserved in the labyrinthian libraries of Nature's codes.

Every light-being is a flame-seed of the new history, an essential current in the galactic seas. Billions of planets may be seen as granules of sand, as individuals in various stages of refinement upon the shores of eternity — a vast chemistry simultaneously encompassing the past, present and future. The alchemical chef, our Maestro, blends our every enzyme in the seething cauldron of existence.

As each raindrop is a unique jewel in a liquid world, we are our own singular nature; in recognizing our particular value, we recognize ourselves. There are so many opaque veils to deter us, seductions that offer paths of self-importance, tempting us to put our energy outward before it goes inward.

Each of us is a flame within the eternal kiln, casting an essential ray into infinity.

How does a geyser explode without the condensation of its source? Our light is beamed from our inner ecology and self-knowledge. By accepting and respecting our individuality, we give ourselves the freedom and space essential for our inherent nature to blossom.

Microcosm: Bird Feet

While walking on the beach, I notice tiny bird feet have imprinted the sand. Next to this trail are dog and then human footprints. Next to the human footprints are tidepools with black-vested snails crawling about among brightly colored starfish. And there on the beach, I recognize a diversity of form, of creature, in the musical scores of the wind's dance imprinted in the sands. The liquid breath of existence, in its diversified patterns, dances its evanescent choreography in its own geography.

Let us give ourselves the wings, the right to be free spirits; give our roots their flight. May we comprehend our deepest nature, its relationship to the Whole as we weave our fabric of destiny into the Vast Loom. It is our survival.

an ever-wider beam

As cyber-bats
And earthly-nauts
We sonar beam
Our flight

Suspended threads
Spun resilient
From the dome
Of infinity's web

The balance of our rays
Casts trampolines of light

The symbiosis of
Antennae transmits
An ever-wider beam

"Riding the Quantum Wave"

CHAPTER 10

EDGEWALKING:

THE ACROBAT IN

PARADISE

TAROT:
THE ACE OF WANDS
This ace stands for initiative, courage, and willingness to take risks, as well as enthusiasm and élan. The Ace of Wands also frequently indicates the area of central self-fulfillment…. According to the fire element [represented by the Wands], this can be a matter of strengthening our will, our convictions, and our moral strength, or it can be related to other inner maturity and growth processes. Furthermore, the Ace of Wands means an affirmation of life, optimism, and high spirits.

I thrive as an aesthetic explorer, an inventor, disinterested in the political games of society, except to study them. Bored with mediocrity, ignited by the nascent forces that be, I neither adapt to nor adopt the ideologies of others. As an acrobat of the unknown, I delight in the discoveries inherent in being an edgewalker. To experience the poetry of the instant is to be a ballerina reaching into the Beyond.

I walk the razor's edge, the diaphanous membrane between one reality and another. My invisible guide provides me with both all and nothing. I withdraw from will, from mind fabrications. The vast energy, the effortless becomes my current. I tightrope walk the chasms, the ravines of wailing fears and bottomless void. Nothing is secure except that which is given up; all else atrophies in the clasp of fear.

Depending on our attitude, tension may be thought of as an invasion of peace or as an essential force. The tension that ennobles survival, ennobles me. As I travel on my astral trapeze, balancing my dance in the unknown, Nature's Laws smile back in the translatable symbols of the profound.

Nothing is secure except that which is given up; all else atrophies in the clasp of fear.

To live the invisible is to treat life as an experiment. Our inventions, their outcomes, are at risk, but also is our vulnerable state of being that made them possible. As quoted in the book, *The Grand Eccentrics*, "Invention is the most difficult task for the human mind."

May we metabolize the poetic as our reality. To walk uplifted in the world requires both balance and vigilance. When we travel psychic space, let us have clear skies and lucid perception to recognize the ego disguises, the seductions and distractions that constantly tempt us off our path.

To live the precipice between life and death is a precarious balance of living the edges, our consciousness navigating from the fires of experience. It takes as much courage to live this way as it does to fight on the very battlefields of war. As acrobats in the cosmic gymnasium, the more we dare to live the edges, the further our stretch into the Divine.

courage

I refused the circus
                    now I walk my own tightrope
                              outside the massive tent
My white arms flung wind-spread
                              into spacelessness
No shouldering branch
                    or supporting breeze for balance
Vertiginous amidst such vastness
                    I spiral around and around
                              unfurling into vacuous spheres
I grasp hollow air
                    wavering in the currents
I reach the center of my rope
                    stretched so high — so taut
                              only blackness meets my fall

Then I stop, and remember
                    performing inside that doomed tent
                         jumping through hoops
                              riding nude upon prancing ponies
Exulting
          from rows of eyes
                    mirroring applause
                              blinking, clapping
Reflecting their psychedelic creation of me
I belonged to those
                    who didn't
                              couldn't know me and
I could not claim a self, myself until
I walked my own tightrope
                         realizing
                              over there
                                   in that airless tent
                              Performers are encapsulated
                                   dazed
                                        within stunting acts

"Cosmic Cartoon"

CHAPTER 11

THE PAGEANTRY

OF EXISTENCE

THE
I CHING:
[FROM 11. T'AI /
PEACE, RE. NINE IN
THE THIRD PLACE]

Everything on earth is subject to change. Prosperity is followed by decline; this is the eternal law on earth. Evil can indeed be held in check but not permanently abolished. It always returns. This conviction might induce melancholy, but it should not; it ought only to keep us from falling into illusion....

As long as a man's inner nature remains stronger and richer than anything offered by external fortune, as long as he remains inwardly superior to fate, fortune will not desert him.

Our lives are movies in which we seriously believe the roles we play. This great theater of diverse characters is an outrageous pageantry of endless absurdities. When we perceive reality from the Overview, we see the humor, the irony of this outlandish theater we inhabit. When we are misled by ego, prejudice, belief systems or any fanaticism, seriousness can be dangerous. Wisdom gives us a glimpse between the seams, beyond the facade of appearance.

In living our Tao, we may behold this glorious theater, this playground of experiment as an eternal odyssey. Aware of the humor, we spread the pollen of paradise, singing of the outrageous. Being brave is a full-time sport; we must stand being outcasts, uniting with other renegades, other anarchists of the caged spirit.

Life has me reeling in its senselessness, its contradictions. I throw up my hands, my lantern of mind to the stars, transcending the need for explanations, the cause and effect. "I don't search; I find," as Picasso said. I let life reveal itself to me as a flower does to its pollinator. I unravel the threads of my gossamer fabric into unfolding discovery.

I laugh at the cosmic joke, its prismatic poses. I take ideas seriously, yet exhilarate in their annihilation. Humor, lost to ego and pride, is redeemed in wisdom.

infinities unknown

I see the froth of waves,
the crest that rises

I behold life's phenomena,
the drama of its myths

And I understand
that underneath
the gallop of surf, and
beneath the roles we play

Is the wilderness of forces
the dynamics of the mystery,
the Maestro that holds
our puppet strings
from up above to
down below

What we can see
in the froth of waves,
in the story of our hearts
is the ripple and the song
from infinities unknown

When we perceive reality from the Overview, we see the humor, the irony of this outlandish theater we inhabit.

"The Carousel Riders"

TRANSFORMING

THE MUNDANE

THE I CHING:
16. YÜ /
ENTHUSIASM
Because enthusiasm shows devotion to movement, heaven and earth are at its side.... The secret of all natural and human law is movement that meets with devotion.

TAROT:
10 OF PENTACLES
In order to attain inner abundance, alert attentiveness is necessary.... We only have to open our eyes in order to experience what the supposedly gray life can really offer to us.... In the professional field, this means gaining something even from the routine of our everyday work life in order to experience it as a source of inner enrichment.

The ordinary, the mechanized, can be transformed by a change of perception, a vibrancy of spirit. Let us discriminate which emotional shades we paint onto the palette of the everyday. Go softly into the day, calm amidst the turbulent storms of human existence.

I am called to trans-forming. I can live outside of society, but not outside of myself. I spiral dance in the Earth's gymnasium, forever correcting, progressing, with ever-new steps. As poet and friend, David Wayne Dunn reminds me, "life is an eternal beginning."

Our challenge is both to endure and rejoice in that which our natures demand. Although I have shed much of the extraneous, the mundane has a demanding voice, requiring constant attention to the mechanical, the money matters, the etceteras. Is Nature weary of being the creator, as we creatures are? Ah, if we could only rest, recognize the futility of trying, and know how to be a peaceful day.

Routine is essential to the progress of our life's work. Yet, with imaginative exploration, most situations can be enhanced. When we are inspired, even the mundane, the technology of repetition can be a quietly exhilarating meditation.

the liquid winds of poetry

Scorched fields of maize gasp
Flooded in dust and sun
Ghost thistles leer
Where a breeze of wild flowers waltzed
Dense air is heavy to breathe

A seared heart
Silent of poetry
Stalks the immobile riverbed

Where is the music
That danced the river
Sang the stone
Pulsed the verse
Petaled flowers?

When will surge again
The liquid winds of poetry;
The forms of meaning
Sculpt from void

The ordinary,
the mechanized,
can be transformed
by a change of
perception, a
vibrancy of spirit.

"Inner Temple"

CHAPTER 13

BUILDING

A PERSONAL

ARCHITECTURE

In the gradual process of enlightenment, theories, philosophies, belief systems may guide us, another's words may validate, but only our own experience will dawn the light of our inward sun, illuminating our unique path to the paradise within.

Observing uncivilization's systems and exploitive politics reveals the need for us, as explorers, to manifest our ideals. Perhaps this focus is particularly necessary for the outsider, the spiritual creator, yet each of us holds those possibilities within. In this time of ever-accelerating chaos, when we and our planet are further than ever from sanity, birthing our own personal mythology is essential. If our priorities come from our highest intention, we can architect philosophic systems that reflect an inner policy of refinement.

Fear chooses prejudice over philosophy. The ego-responses of prejudice, judgment, jealousy, competition and greed are to be shed. From the very marrow of our existence, let us craft our own spiritual architecture. Why live in someone else's house? Only we can build our inner temples, tend the gardens of our inner ecology.

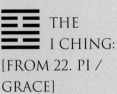 THE
I CHING:
[FROM 22. PI /
GRACE]
By contemplating the forms existing in the heavens we come to understand time and its changing demands. Through contemplation of the forms existing in human society it becomes possible to shape the whole world.

TAROT:
QUEEN OF WANDS
On the level of consciousness this card means that we open ourselves to a power in life that supports warmth and lightheartedness as well as courage and initiative in us. It says that we no longer let ourselves be driven by meager practical considerations or float without a will. It shows the willingness to actively create our own lives and live them according to our own ideals.

...only our own experience will dawn the light of our inward sun, illuminating our unique path to the paradise within.

~

May each of us cultivate our own personal mythology, emanating from a cosmic connection to all things. Then like spiders, we can spin our interpretations, new comprehensions, into the grand suspended embroidery, balancing more easily in the unknown.

songs to the tao

Oh, Tao that is my ocean
I listen to your sound

Oh, Tao of which I'm a current
I yield to your liquid roar

Oh, Tao of intricate fabric
I add my special threads

Oh, Tao who moves me beyond
I bless you for my life

Oh, Tao that guides my flow
I yield to harmony's way

Oh, Tao of subtle meanings
I vow to notice and hear

Oh, Tao of Nature's ways
I live from your roots

Oh, Tao of ultimate meanings
I am all that you are, yet nothing

Oh, Tao with whom I'm One
Embrace me as intimately
        as I can bear

"The Path"

CHAPTER 14

TRUSTING

THE TAO

Why toil with concepts when the worthwhile occurs from a more discreet design? I let my will go as a stream, yielding to life's rocks, allowing the natural order to take its course, moving only when it feels right. I offer my visions to Providence, where all things are decoded according to the Grand Intelligence. To try to control life, subverts its flow. Nature thrives from the greater urge of evolution, to which I yield.

We grow toward the sun as our own unique beams, trusting life's flow. In touch on this deep, expansive level, we will survive, prosper as "life's will," as the weed that cracks and sprouts through the freeway.

The saying "The meek shall inherit the Earth" can be interpreted as meaning that through lack of coercion, all is won because there is no battle to be fought. All is One and all is won. If we yield to the *Is*, we are *Its* inheritor. The person is great who understands his or her position in perspective to the whole.

A wind sweeps my life energies into a harvest, a quantum wave. I ride this momentum beyond what I can know. The Great Wind and the harvesting of all I have lived recreate me as an effulgent fountain.

Each moment is an embryo, a nucleus of possibility to be cultivated by courage and faith, then released to flower.

THE
I CHING:
1. CHIEN / THE
CREATIVE
Here it is shown that the way to success lies in apprehending and giving actuality to the way of the universe (tao), which, as a law running through end and beginning, brings about all phenomena in time.

TAROT:
2 OF PENTACLES
The 2 of Pentacles... shows that we can adapt ourselves to the currents of life, passing through the heights and depths without much difficulty.... It represents...the humble wisdom of the fool who has found his or her way back to the simple, uninhibited contemplation of a child after an arduous process of perception.

In Oneness is the ultimate suspension.

Let us be as mystics, fed from the silent language, the uncontrived, the untrammeled dialogue absorbed in our marrow. May we walk as chosen ones, in the Tao of our deeper existence, beholding our lives as our own miracle, in dialogue with the Divine. In the ecstasy of metabolizing poetry, we become dancers of the Higher Order.

To be friends with the Unknown is to rest as easily on our trapeze, our gossamer connection, as on the Earth. In Oneness is the ultimate suspension.

Microcosm: The Infinite Energy

In the late afternoon, I float in the tropical mountain lake above the birds. I offer myself to life in a renewed way. I remember that the greatest enemy of life is fear. Why be afraid to live when we can give ourselves to the multidimensional? Then we can breathe with its contractions, do without doing. I offer my being to the infinite energy that is mine in that resonance of wholeness.

writing poetry

Let the feelings flow
from pen to page

Let the unknown
lift you in its winds,
be a lullaby in the breeze

Let the moon's gaze
answer your questions, and
the sun pervade

Let the symphony
of all existence
enter your ears

Let your busy mind
go to the gods

The surf below
awaits the new wave

And I,
with my pen,
live the pulse,
weave its patterns
upon the page

"Reverence for Nature"

CHAPTER 15

THE LANGUAGE

OF NATURE

The signals of Nature's voice resonate as my own.
The omniscient Shadow pulses its oracles within me.
A symbiotic dialogue ripples through my streams,
murmuring to me of the great cosmic abstractions.
I feel at one with all that is and has ever been.
The vast, wild Eternal is the seas surging, revealing
endlessly new psyche-vistas. The geometric granules
of interrelationship are uncoded.

The metaphors of Nature's omens speak from the
unconditioned, the origin, and thus are the most direct.
Our questings may be guided by the myriad symbols of
Nature's voice, pulsing the oracular codes. The meaning
of who we are is imprinted invisibly within granules of
sand, within massive mountains. When I experience this
space beyond concept, I see myself reflected in Nature's
climes, in the phenomena I behold.

I see through the creatures' eyes and in studying them
rediscover Nature's primal laws. My insights are inspired
by discussions with the wise, and also by observing the
baby field mouse who can hang by its tail, performing
astonishing acrobatic feats.

I live in unfolding wonder, experiencing life's contradictions.
The more simply I live, the more the silent languages
reveal, uncoding the mysterious messages of DNA.

TAROT:
II THE HIGH
PRIESTESS
*...For a period of time...
we turn our attention to
the subconscious and the
innermost images of our
souls, let ourselves be
guided by creative
phantasies and dreams
or delve down into the
shadowy depths to lift
the veil that covers the
mysterious wisdom of
the High Priestess,
rediscovering the ancient
truths....*

I see through the
creatures' eyes
and in studying
them rediscover
Nature's primal
laws.

I wish to be a creature of Nature without affectation,
in dialogue with its arcane powers. In my intimacy
with the vast wilderness I inhabit, discoveries are born.
I offer myself to life's bounty, as a wave to the infinite
seas, awaiting the subtle guidance of Nature.

Microcosm: The Silent Language Returns
Today is radiant. Every step on Wreck Beach redesigns
another wonder, a meditation, an I Ching hexagram,
another law about life expressed as a reflection in the
tidepools. I hear the divine voices, the sound of the
breezes rippling the trees, the white lyrics of Wreck
Beach, the coves of intimacy everywhere murmuring.

I watch the shimmer of the wind's breath play the instrument
of the seas, adding to the endless symphony of which I too
am a part. My sensibilities are bathed clear in the winds.

All that has ever been and all I have ever known reflects
in the undulating seas. The subtleties and textures of
the silent language return to my gardens. They brim in
my circulation.

The evening tides pulse as mine. Lunar images enamel
the shimmering ebony body of the sea. I drift into the other
world, the home of the ancient teachings, the undisturbed
spirit world, in cadence with sublime intuition. Here,
I reconnect with the Gnostics, the deeper healings, the
ancient wisdom.

collage of inscapes

The liquid pulse of ancient seas
Pounds upon my shores within

High tides circulate my sands
Tiny granules — bits of mind
Shoreline patterns redesign
Bridges form in floods of vision
Metabolize once foreign isles

The untamed suns of violet
Dazzle through my eyes
Prisms of particles reflect
Swirl in changing constellations

In the wild heavens
Of my night skies

The Formless in ever-moving form

"Must Flee the City"

CHAPTER 16

THE RESTORATIVE POWER OF WILDERNESS

THE I CHING: 2. K'UN / THE RECEPTIVE

Nature's richness lies in its power to nourish all living things; its greatness lies in its power to give them beauty and splendor. Thus it prospers all that live.

TAROT: III THE EMPRESS

The Empress personifies the inexhaustible power of nature, with which she continues to bring forth new life.

Wilderness is the great integrator, restorer of seed, where the weariness of the world is erased in uncontrived space. The higher the frequency, the greater the order. In the seminal silence of wilderness, we may embrace peace. When we honor Nature as ourselves, we inherit the Earth.

We need not separate from the endless power of Nature, of ourselves. As we imbibe the fresh mountain stream after the storms, we feel its pure current inherent in each of us. As we emerge into our more refined natures, we drop the boomerangs of self-division, the burden of judgment. Our origin is returned, before defense, before conditioning. Oneness dissolves separateness.

Microcosm: The Intimate Dialogue

Living simply, I experience mellifluous days of inhaling Nature in the balm of contentment. I sink into my gardens at home, feeling the green grasses bloom through my being. I am in dialogue with the earth, metabolizing its

> Wilderness is the great integrator, restorer of seed, where the weariness of the world is erased in uncontrived space.

arcane power. Damp grasses soothe my soul; rages that once burned, abandoned to the flames, now yield in my garden's emerald green embrace. I thrive in my garden of delicate tendril, enjoying the freedom, the deeper soil of my soul. I gaze into Nature's wondrous complexity, into her countless leaves, sculptured limbs. My sensibilities are finely tuned, receptive to the intimate dialogue, a drumming of the poetic heart.

The rhythms of moving sunlight dance upon the seas as I wander the living light of day. The vast body of the undulating seas ripples in the effervescence of aqua music. Gold light rides the breath of the breeze. The sunlight beams deep into my neck. The gifts of this magnificent Earth pour into me. I am an Indian, indigenous to just being.

The tides blossom into vast white birds' wings on the shores below. Listening to the birds, I hear the sounds of the infinite and am released into the cosmic symphony. Traveling the distant realms impassions me; I enter the playground of dreams, feeling the peace of the ancients. Dissolving into the white sound of silence, into the tide's urge, I ride the rhythms that bore infinity, that breathed the first emerald into form.

As the quixotic climates exert their wild energies over this land, I am transported to the Divine Ground of Being. The endless worlds of the miraculous break upon my shores, as the winged tides below.

Oceans of fog tumble down Cone Peak's ravines. I inhale the mist of enshrouded madrone and am revivified. Why is it so easy to forget what we need most: the health of the wilderness as our own?

Aligned with the Neptunian forms, the seas, the clouds, I am at one with the wild creatures, with the numinous, animating forces. I am stillness again, regenerated.

the shoreless spheres

I'm drawn to the shoreless spheres
To where the wild things live
In migrating rhythms

Where seagulls glide vagrant tides
To the jet contour of lone cormorant
Where wilderness unravels tangled root
Inhaling beyond framed self
Where pulses current one harmony,
Igniting the endless fabric
To where the wild things live and die

Where the will of man
Does not impose
Alibis of purpose:
Goals that stomp upon
The ephemeral dunes of wind-spun sand,
The shoreless spheres of mind

Ebb — suspension — flow
To where the wild things live

"Taurean Moon"

CHAPTER 17

NATURE'S CYCLES

⚏ THE
I CHING:
[FROM 16. YÜ /
ENTHUSIASM]

*The inviolability of
natural law rests on this
principle of movement
along the line of least
resistance. These laws
are not forces external to
things but represent the
harmony of movement
immanent in them.
That is why the celestial
bodies do not deviate
from their orbits and why
all events in nature occur
with fixed regularity.*

Emotional reality can be as changeable as the climates.
Our seasons revolve; so too may our interpretations.
The endless cycles are to be viewed from a broad
perspective. When we see through the Cosmic Eye,
our perception is holographic.

Chaos is as essential in the natural order as is harmony.
The cycles are endless; they become one and the same
if looked at with detachment. If we endure the frost of
winter, our spring will come. Nature is our highest
technology; we can but yield to her seasons as our own.

Harmony requires the balancing of all worlds. The Earth's
soul pulses through our center, into infinity. We are at
one with the myriad cycles of planets, stars, and moons.
Let our homage be to the galactic order, within. May our
odyssey be to live from an intimate integrity, to aspire
to the sun as walking trees.

A wave of tenderness, of levitation, sweeps me into
revelation, into a microscopic view of the instant. The
sycamore leaves fall, a palette of wildflowers blossoms,
biting winds wail to the endless oceans. I am dissolved
into the rhythms of this evanescent ballet. This exquisite
profundity is lost in an instant to the ever-changing, yet
forever beheld within Nature's invisible strings, beheld
by the essence from which all life springs.

Pause in motion is one of Nature's basic rhythms.

In the autumn, the gold manes of a stallion-surf spray the air. The velocity of Nature's urge is in my marrow. A great wind lifts me beyond the chaos of violence, its tearing force. As liberated light, I ascend, the wind in my ears, in my fingertips' quickened touch. I watch the autumn leaves change and fall. So will I re-alchemize in constant preparation for my next season of being.

In the winter, I have the need to withdraw, as does the dormant seed. I regenerate in the primal deeper caves, detaching from extraneous habits. As the sea's tides wash over my toes, I let the waters of the unconscious bathe my mind. I bask in quietude, the sublime nurturance. Winter gives birth to solitude, to rejuvenation.

In the spring, the Core of the Universe whispers through my ears. I let my roots, as anchors, bed in the storm-wet soil. I breathe the blossoming scents. Although the seeds are yet to manifest, I feel their intention as my own. When their soft, downy tendrils begin the promise of new life, every part is vulnerable, not to be trampled.

In the dryness of summer, sunny, lazy days are filled with insect-eating swallows and summer personalities. I travel into the imagination, into the warble of the bird's ancient song. I imbibe the fragrance of magnolia blossoms, the breezes of heated ambrosia, and walk on. Pause in motion is one of Nature's basic rhythms. As human beings, may we also pause in motion, restoring our flaming plumes in aqua waters.

Each day is a weaving in the continuum, an integration that composes the chords of time into an eternal symphony. I move freely without self-imposed will. Each action I take is ignited from the Universal. An ecology of being prevails. Now is the season for my soil to be nourished, for the new seeds of my birthing spirit to grow.

at a different time

My waves rise red
in the moon's winter breath
The silver tides
do not cool the rage

The raving winds
of aspiration's blaze
have consumed
my tree's lair

The crown is bare,
the seeds invaded
The winter's season
has been subverted

Can the spring to come
then be my winter?
Can the day's morn
be instead my night's sleep?

Will Nature let me rearrange
my cycles and concerns
at a different time
from hers?

"After Chagall"

CHAPTER 18

SYNCHRONICITY

Nature, its ever re-alchemizing stable of forces, doesn't bother with our simulations of belief, rationality and the rest of our strivings to grasp The Mystery. Meaning is to be found in the subtle, refined textures of Nature's language, in synchronicity, in the random events that change our lives. If we recognize that we are forces of Nature, guided by our self-knowledge, our comprehension of the Higher Order, we will be led by an ever-expanding consciousness, simultaneously personal and universal. In this clarity, Nature's laws reveal the fundamentals essential to evolve. Each creature's survival relies on what it understands about itself and the world.

If Nature is observed in quietude, the synchronicities that reveal the greater truth can be seen, translated into the meaningful from the insignificant. Each rock that falls into the cosmic seas adds its ripples to the endless web of infinity's currents.

That which is ours, comes to us, although anxiety-driven will may block this benevolence and invite deprivation. Everything that is truly essential has come my way riding a figurine of mist; I was there and so was "it." That "it" is the random design of the Vast Loom, allowing us glimpses of its paradox and absurdity, of its ironic demeanor, of its multifaceted countenance. We may receive what we ask for in unrecognizable disguises.

There in the wilderness, where white heat blazes, where the sun of my dial is a magnet for the unexpected, lives the whim-filled chance called Life. There, the incidental may be recognized for its meaning. Miracles may become

---

THE I CHING: 46. SHÊNG / PUSHING UPWARDS

The pushing upward of the good elements encounters no obstruction and is therefore accompanied by great success. The pushing upward is made possible not by violence, but by modesty and adaptability. Since the individual is borne along by the propitiousness of the time, he advances.

TAROT: PAGE OF PENTACLES

The Page of Pentacles proclaims an opportunity that is offered to us, an impulse that crosses our path.... Plans take form, intentions turn into reality. Ideas that have up to now tended to just be mind games are turned into action by this impetus.

> In the profundity of the silent language, symbolism is multilingual.

visible in this dimension, where fabricated reality dissolves. Perspectives expand as the Universal becomes more transparent.

In the profundity of the silent language, symbolism is multilingual. I notice which thoughts, objects and people occur in synchronicity, beyond our self-concoctions. Let the experiments of each second have their wildness, their leopard spots in Sufi dance, their atoms in celebration.

When the magic of synchronicity manifests, we receive a glimpse of the Grand Design, which at other times lies hidden.

Microcosm: A Humming Synchronicity

Every day has been perfect and ecstatic, tuned into the resonance of a humming synchronicity. Each day surfs the metabolic forces of history; it's as if I am peering back from the future into the present reel of myth.

The significance of occurrences is a continual wonder. I have only to love, trust, rest and the universe cushions my soul, answers me in its deepest sapience. My energy is like a great wind that has found resonant worlds to travel. Through this thrust, I feel a strong sense of personal destiny and the consequent interlinking with those vital others.

glass world

I see through the force universal,
the fertility of all

A miraculous unfolding of synchronicity
revealing endless faces of serendipity,
interlinking causality

The DNA code manifests
in the subtle realms

The universe is in dialogue
with my deeper whispers

I yield,
allow its breath to live me,
receive this force beyond
Be it, embrace it,
let the fertility of core
feed my action, words

Who am I in the face
of this great shadow?
Who am I as I am swept
beyond self, further every second?

The unknown reveals
the synchronicities of destiny,
the links that speak
of the DNA of the invisible

All that must be
is here within,
mirrored without
A resplendent glass world
of prismatic reflection

"Transparent World"

CHAPTER 19

CAUSALITY

The causes we find for occurrences are often formed from bias, defense and anxiety. Our genetics exert a basic influence. In understanding our given physiology and temperament, we become more flexible and thus more able to shape effects.

The game of cause and effect may be both exhaustive and futile. In our attempts to make sense of life, we often search for answers with a preconditioned mind. Psychology is one way to analyze causes for certain behavior, yet usually the cause is not found solely in its behavioral symptom. The origin may be the voice of the betrayed soul seeking recognition from the darkness shading its face.

Beyond our conditioning, beyond the obvious, is the Vast Electronic Wave of which we are intricate currents. We exist as One, as do cause and effect. As everything contributes to cause and effect, only by examining the whole can we offer solutions.

Microcosm: My Art
The synchronicity of cause and effect is analogous to the process of creating art. Each line drawn creates yet another form, which then may beget yet another. Light gives dark its form. As in our living, elements that appear to be in juxtaposition are, in actuality, of each other.

THE
I CHING:
[FROM TA CHUAN /
THE GREAT
TREATISE]
In their alternation and reciprocal effect, the two fundamental forces (yin/yang) serve to explain all the phenomena in the world. Nonetheless, there remains something that cannot be explained in terms of the interaction of these forces, a final why. This ultimate meaning of tao is the spirit, the divine, the unfathomable in it, that which must be revered in silence.

the oeuvre of origin

Emotions may pluck
if let to play
the strings of one's violin

Quixotic as notes in a song
climes of the sky
or colors of the meadow

Beyond the cover
of illusion
behold the hidden eye:
the oeuvre of origin

Enter the seed
heart of the weed
inside the color
deep in the core
is where the secret thrives

There, one will
not find deception.

The synchronicity
of cause and effect
is analogous to
the process of
creating art.

"Café Van Gogh"

CHAPTER 20

THE RELATIVITY

OF REALITY

As said in the Talmud, "Things are not the way *they* are; they are the way *we* are."

Depending on our vantage point, on our capacity for comprehensive perception, we experience numerous truths, interpretations of reality. With every event, there is a diversity of experience and perception; what is truth for one is not necessarily truth for another. When we carefully examine the truth of what we perceive, we may discover that it does not endure. The essence may be in what we can not see rather than in our interpretation of its appearance. Underlying the stories we tell, is the autonomy of Nature's laws.

Fanatics assume their ideas are fact, that there is only one reality. Their belief systems prevent new perspectives. Although opinions are merely a reflection of the person who has them, they may still exert a suffocating influence, robbing others of their own authority.

Misunderstanding arises from the assumption that there is only one reality. The perspectives of people with different orientations to life will usually conflict. If we address only the limit of appearance, how can we agree on the deeper meaning? It is unlikely we can share a reality with others if our assumptions come from misconception and ignorance of the variables of the greater reality.

THE
I CHING:
[FROM 20. KUAN /
CONTEMPLATION
(VIEW) RE. SIX IN
THE THIRD PLACE]
We no longer look outward to receive pictures that are more or less limited and confused, but direct our contemplation upon ourselves in order to find a guideline for our decisions. This self-contemplation means the overcoming of naive egotism in the person who sees everything solely from his own standpoint. He begins to reflect and in this way acquires objectivity.

TAROT:
X THE WHEEL OF
FORTUNE
According to the way in which we approach our destiny, we experience The Wheel of Fortune either as an expression of our powerlessness and helplessness or as an indication of a knowledge of life through which we can grow and mature.

Our interpretations of reality are like clothes we wear so we won't shiver in the Void.

Thus endless deliberation occurs without reconciliation or progress. Unitive knowledge is possible only when every viewpoint is considered, valued as a piece of the cosmic puzzle. If there were only one possible viewpoint, telescopes would have stationary lenses.

I devoted many years to studying the question, "What is reality?" Which facet of the kaleidoscope shall I choose as my lens? With the realization that reality is as one perceives it, comes a certain grace in living. Einstein scientifically informed us that reality is relative, depending on our vantage point. He had hoped his discovery would spawn a *new way of thinking*.

My life feels constricted when I lose touch with this holographic view of reality. As we accumulate experience we may gain perspective, and thus more comprehension, revealing new vistas to the skies of our minds. As myriad revolving prisms, let us give each facet of our crystalline becoming its view.

I like examining many interpretations of life, later freeing them to the winds, taking a deep breath of a fresh integration. Then I may wonder why I held on so long. Our interpretations of reality are like clothes we wear so we won't shiver in the Void. The challenge is to divest ourselves of the superfluous.

Microcosm: Art Translates Life

My art precedes my consciousness. When my work becomes a struggle, I find I need to expand my perceptions. My liberation often comes from turning a painting upside down and approaching it from every angle. To live life fully, to be creative, requires a kaleidoscopic awareness, a multidimensional approach.

beyond duality

Perceptions
  perspectives
    change form
      from one's stance

In the vortex
  of mountain river
    dualities dissolve

When fresh water
  blends with brine,
    sweet and salty
      become one

As boulders mark time
  within eternal space,
    I travel the storm-wind,
      rhythm's scores of existence

I am but a seagull's cry
  a sound in resonance
    a wave in ancient code unfurling

"*The Building of Realities*"

CHAPTER 21

BUILDING

REALITIES

As I gaze from the mountain lake high above the seas, into the mists, the unexplored skies, I see into life. I peer into its fundamental meanings, into my own, into how we virtualize reality. Suddenly, life appears as a series of projected images created by my mind, orchestrated by passion — an endless reel of universal forces mirrored in others, in myself, in the world.

In living beyond the density of self-limitation, we can create our own myth. The instrument of our beings may conduct either our likes or dislikes, our paradise or the misery of distortion. Whatever I envision will be my mythology for manifestation. Awareness of the power of this realization seems to blow like a great wind through me. We can fly above the birds if we so choose. Our dreams are spun from the finest filigree of our most powerful feelings, thus they are the strongest, the most vulnerable, the engine-creators with inexhaustible fuel.

It is our relationship to our deeper nature that is outer-reflected. I take responsibility, discarding games of demon projections and sabotage as my alibis. I realize others bring their own reality and dynamics, but when I am attuned to my higher intention, if another energy is discordant, I can navigate toward harmony, rather than become entangled. Corruption dissolves when we are in communion with the silent lake of ourselves reflected.

THE
I CHING:
1. CH'IEN / THE
CREATIVE POWER

The beginning of all things lies still in the beyond in the form of ideas that have yet to become real. But the Creative…has power to lend form to these archetypes of ideas.

TAROT:
I THE MAGICIAN

The Magician represents… skillfulness, self-confidence and actively creating your own life…. The extraordinary influential powers and effectiveness shown by The Magician are based upon the secret of deep harmony between the conscious and the unconscious. It is only the inner certainty, which then occurs, that is capable of moving mountains.

Our dreams are
the songs our
hearts play to
our souls.

As we think, so we are; perhaps *thinking* we have a problem is the problem. With myriad perspectives comes the necessity for us to discriminate. As Benjamin DeCasseres has reminded me, this most essential capacity comes from first knowing ourselves. We can only discriminate when we are in accord with our essential rhythms and from there, develop our own philosophy.

If we so reform ourselves, we can reform society. Our society's habits are outworn, leading to self-imprisonment. Rather than be the ignorant victim of exploitive systems, it is essential that we create our own structures.

Our dreams are the songs our hearts play to our souls. They must be transfused by our very bloodstreams to become living entities. Some of my dreams have emerged; others are yet to be realized. When I complete the dream's form in my blood, it will manifest. I trust the vision, the dream, the circulation of its body and light in cosmic time. The dreams of my existence beat deep and eternally in the resonance of endless birth, emanating when their light of consciousness is available. After their conception they gestate in the radiance that warms their molecular engines, sometimes requiring many lifetimes, or manifesting instantaneously should destiny demand. According to Eric Drexler, we are our own nanotechnology, "engines of creation."

Because our theater of existence requires projection to exist, why engage in mediocrity? Why not create the inspirational, the ecstatic? Poets, artists and friends of the culture are called to sing from their greatest joy, and if of their noblest nature, Earth can recreate its Garden of Eden.

spirit-song

The lullabies our souls sing
to soothe our saddened brow
may be just stories
and for some, just made up lies

But without our stories
and without our lullabies
the violin is left unplayed
and our ears betrayed
become quite cold

Death is just a corpse
and love bitter illusion,
if our woven myth
is not our spirit-song

"Parroting Oneself"

CHAPTER 22

ATOMS

MIRROR

ATOMS

When we contemplate the number of atoms in existence, we begin to glimpse the scope of life's mathematical equations. With the emergence of each atom, another possibility for diversification is born, and with diversification comes mutation, evolution's promise.

Our systems constantly clone themselves on a cellular level and, similarly, on emotional and spiritual levels, although only certain facets may be visible. As Nature's seeds, our inner technology is replicated in the exterior. We recreate ourselves through our memes*, our actions, our cars. As copy machines, we multiply what we are in many forms, without conscious discrimination.

I notice the hummingbird with its unique needle-like beak, which mirrors the fluted form of the flower that offers it nectar. My paintings reflect my molecular energy. A painting *is* the painter; a book, its author. We create what we are. The harmonious marriage of platonic forms reveals a mystery that is perfection itself.

This principle implies that like attracts like. Because we emit particular vibrations, we tune into similar frequencies,

THE
I CHING:
[FROM 1. CH'IEN /
THE CREATIVE RE.
NINE IN THE FIFTH
PLACE]

Confucius says about this line: "Things that accord in tone vibrate together. Things that have affinity in their inmost natures seek one another. Water flows to what is wet, fire turns to what is dry.... What is born of heaven feels related to what is above. What is born of earth feels related to what is below. Each follows its kind."

TAROT:
XI JUSTICE

On the everyday level... [this card] says that we experience our surroundings as our echo and will be confronted with the results of our actions, be they good or bad.... This card expresses a high degree of personal responsibility.

* see glossary

Meaning vanishes without passion, the igniter of the inanimate.

attracting our own resonance. The number of channels we have open will determine how myriad our reception. As cosmic instruments, we are unique transmitters emitting our own sound, discordant or harmonious.

The more we recognize our likeness reflected in all other forms, the less separation exists. Unity arises in this recognition of our sameness and the essentiality of our differences. All that we see in the ever-changing skies, is Earth's life reflected. Our energy is forever multiplied, involuntarily. All we need to do is breathe, and atoms mirror atoms*. As above, so below.

A related principle is that the macrocosm* is contained in the microcosm. The pulse of infinity is contained in one rain drop. Like an endless fractal, the universe has everything within it and within everything is the universe. The granule of sand speaks of its beach, the tides chant of eternity. A drop of water is no less significant because it is the microcosm, nor is the ocean greater because it is the macrocosm. Neither exists without the other. As we are to our grain of sand, so we are to our beach.

As we are microcosms of the macrocosm, hierarchical systems may enslave our lives. Cops, robbers, nurses, judges, tyrants and slaves are replicated both within and outside ourselves. Thus, without the flexibility of consciousness, freedom can become a wistful illusion.

Just as our immune system is relentlessly fighting off bacteria and disease, so the flux and flow of life and death can be felt within and observed without. Volcanoes, droughts, all human and natural conditions are duplicated within the individual as in the universe. Some forces are in disguise, but their effect reveals their dynamics. Throughout history we have had viral predators such as Adolf Hitler and Saddam Hussein whose poisons

* see glossary

fuel the flames of paranoia. Their brutality uninhibits other killers, who in turn may also destroy the cellular fabric of society. The fear they engender in others pumps excess adrenaline into the planet organism, into its people. Do those agents of destruction appear in certain cycles of our planet's immune system? Can we think of these destructive forces objectively, as externalized functions of the Earth's immune system, as in auto-immune disease? As we change our thinking, perhaps these human seeds of violence will wither, be ineffective, as in the Sixth Dimension where death as we know it does not exist. Why are we surprised to see so much violence in the world when within our cellular structures the same forces exist?

Microcosm: Inner Reflects Outer Climes

The innate forces within us are expressed as dynamics in the world. The climates of our minds reflect the climates of the universe. From the fountains of our alchemy, we create our own atmosphere and environment. The atmosphere that Wolf* and I create is reflected inside and outside our den. When our natures become alienated, the weather seems to reflect us. Or are we reflecting it? The wind may grow violent, while our shuddering hearts sleep separately. As the currents snarl and tear in myriad directions, so temporarily our souls are wrenched from each other, lost to ominous forces. A ghost inhabits where joy once lived. The *doppelganger* sweeps through like the positive ion winds of the *sirocco,* ruthlessly changing the emotions. Those days we are apart, divided against ourselves, our world becomes barren. The candles lose their glow. Meaning vanishes without passion, the igniter of the inanimate.

In acknowledging Nature as ourselves, we can channel these forces, navigating with sublime intuition.

The harmonious
marriage of
platonic forms
reveals a mystery
that is perfection
itself.

We are the powers of evolution that can only be realized
in understanding Nature as ourselves. The danger
present in Nature's edges, or extremes, is also possible
in our personal experience. When we are engaged in
the extremes of our personal forces, it can be violent or
ecstatic. We can be a river of poison, or a geyser of life.
Perhaps the beginning of awakening is in realizing it is
up to us to move with these forces. In acknowledging
Nature as ourselves, we can channel these forces,
navigating with sublime intuition.

atoms mirror atoms

Leaving the body
Abandoning the finite,

An evolving-revolving vessel
Transmitting pulse from every pore
The ignited senses;
Electrically charged antennae,
Laser threads mercurial
Connecting, fusing
A triumphant penetration
Through Time — Space
Beyond the present — gravity

A personal planet evolving, emerges — Merging
The vessel, the vehicle
Breathes the wing span of the Universe
Living immeasurable vision

Mobilizing another center,
Another gravity
Revolving in one harmony
With the universal order,

The sublime network,
An order interrelating
        all to All

In the profound meaning of Integration
Marrow incenses marrow;
        Atoms mirror atoms;
Magnetic pools of eternal eloquence
In fathomless silence
        So speak

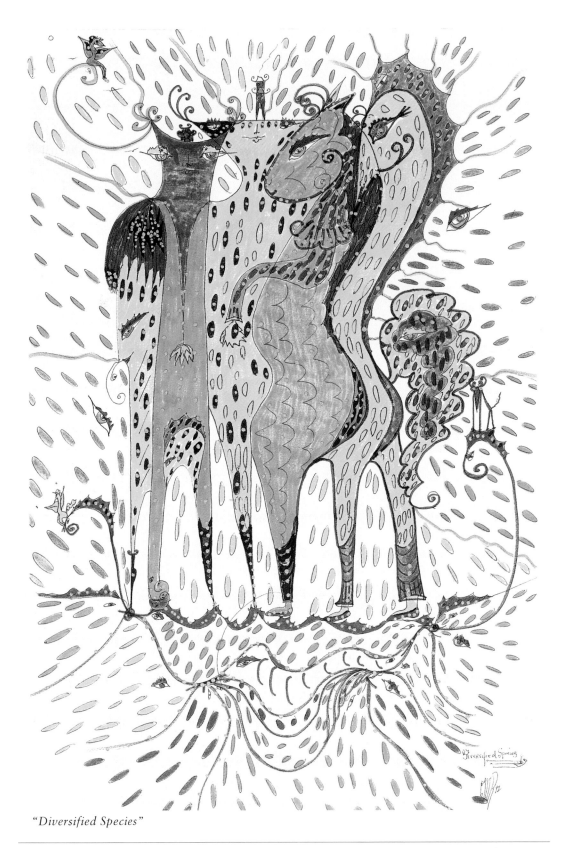

"Diversified Species"

CHAPTER 23

GENETIC

CODES

Each of us may be regarded as a unique blend of chemicals vital to the total organism. Some may be the equivalent of stomach enzymes, others red blood cells and others free radicals. Each of us is a specific and predetermined agent, expressing Nature's chemistry; we express ourselves externally, duplicating our corresponding internal code. Our predetermined genetic function manifests itself in diverse and unique modes of behavior. Through genetic engineering, we can identify some of our unique DNA combinations and have the capacity to provide many of the essentials we need to function at our maximum potential, thus accelerating both our personal and universal ecology. With this ability comes its antagonist, the possibility of automated distortion.

The human species is as peculiar and diverse as the animal or plant kingdom. If we embraced this view, we could be more accepting of each other. If we were to think of ourselves as the instruments of Nature's forces, as vital elements that compose the extravagant alchemy called life, as our own inner biology externalized, we could better appreciate the essentiality of our differences. Each of us in our unique chemistry has a function that will have something essential and unique to offer in the Earth's jungle. The material success of the capitalist could be considered no more essential in function than the tasks of the everyday laborer, or trash-collector. Each is a vital component in the vast organism.

THE
I CHING:
[FROM 15. CH'IEN /
MODESTY]
The destinies of men are subject to immutable laws that must fulfill themselves.

TAROT:
VIII STRENGTH
...the vital energy, courage, and passion of this card is an expression of the reconciliation of the civilized person with his or her animal nature.... This card makes it clear that we cannot aim to hide our instinctual nature behind pallid virtue but should open ourselves much more to encountering the living, sometimes terrifying archaic powers existing in each of us, in order to gradually tame them through loving acceptance and gentle force. When we do this, not only these primordial powers are available to us, but also all of the reserves of strength that we have used up until now to repress these instincts.

The movie of our genetic heredity plays itself out before our astonished and sometimes horrified eyes.

~

As the rigidity of ignorance dissolves, unitive knowledge prevails. As such, we are human tools of the biological complexity, intricate DNA designs of evolution. The movie of our genetic heredity plays itself out before our astonished and sometimes horrified eyes. Our DNA is in a dialogue of correspondence, like an alphabetic code to be translated, for example, through our interrelationships, neuro-politics, worldly affairs, dreams and art. Our partners, lovers, friends are complementary components acting as reflective mirrors to each other in a vast alchemy of interdependent connection.

If we can understand our genetic function-code, we can better accept who we are, recognizing our lovers and friends in relationship to us. We will then put less emphasis on super-ficial response and more on understanding what is innate.

I see that our preordained genetic code, along with our consciousness, directs the films of our essential natures. I used to think psychology alone could rearrange our lives. Now I understand that change is governed by Nature's laws, which expand and guide our awareness.

We carry our humanity wherever we go, no matter how rich, bereft or gifted we are. We can not escape from ourselves; as unique chemical geometries, we play out our given roles in the cosmic theater.

Microcosm: The Recorder Code
What messenger am I from the physics of this metaphor? I am an observer-receiver who records artistic impressions and intuitive states. I take the invisible world of life's dynamics and embroider myself into it; the fabric of me is thus revealed. As a Zen Voidoid*, I offer the poetic metabolism, the film of myself, for development, like the particular species of butterfly which, upon birth, reflects its environment in the patterns of its wings.

---

* see glossary

My art provides an inner-active mirror, revealing in symbolic meaning, archetypal themes, glimpses of our primal souls. Art becomes an aesthetic Rorschach.

Through this recording, I see Nature's process played back in ever-widening awareness. To record and play back this song, lyrically woven within, is my life's work.

As the rigidity of ignorance dissolves, unitive knowledge prevails.

the timeless scrolls of DNA

Within one's molecular labyrinths…
Atomic ladders,
The timeless scrolls
Coiled within, unwind

Filial threads unfurl
Spiral above the bind of gravity
Commute the contained heat
Of the invisible

Evolving self
Transmuting one to All
Transmitting all to One

Each of us is
a specific and
predestined agent
expressing
Nature's chemistry.

"Secret Forest of the Nabis" *

* see glossary

CHAPTER 24

THE

INTERCONNECTEDNESS

OF ALL LIFE

☲ THE
I CHING:
30. LI / THE
CLINGING, FIRE
*Everything that gives light
is dependent on something
to which it clings, in order
that it may continue to
shine. Thus sun and moon
cling to heaven, and grain,
grass, and trees cling to the
earth.... By cultivating
in himself an attitude of
compliance and voluntary
dependence, man acquires
clarity...and finds his place
in the world.*

What constitutes the individual and the organism called Earth, is infinitely complex. Every cell is a part of every other. Our quantum antennae transmit and receive through an invisible network of molecular forces linked with and affecting all of creation. I realize our interdependency in a new way. If we censor or eliminate our receptivity to any facet of humanity, we censor ourselves. If we have compassion for all that exists, we hear the emerald whispers of the universe. The myriad translations of the infinite symphony will reverberate throughout our labyrinthian interiors.

Today, every cell of my being is resonating with this greater understanding of existence. I realize that each person's suffering can be felt by all, and that to evolve, we must be aware of the unified pulse of every creature. Every abuse inflicted on a person or creature, the earth or skies, has a boomerang effect. Every bar that imprisons another wounds everyone. In every denial of feeling is a self-woven grave of numbed sensibilities.

By recognizing our Oneness, our mutual wave of force, we can live our complementary biology, our coded

We are our own self-referencing stars; when guided in harmony with the Whole, we resonate with all of creation.

∼

connectedness. We may accept this intellectually, but only if we experience it directly will we transform.

As human beings, we are in constant flux, as is the planet and its myriad forms of existence. Life is a kiln of mosaics vibrating in the heat, each piece fitting together like a giant jigsaw of diverse design. What is happening to us, the human species, and to our Earth affects intergalactic life in unimaginable ways. We are our own self-referencing stars; when guided in harmony with the Whole, we resonate with all of creation.

Separation is an illusion created by alienated and limited thought. Only through expanding this limited consciousness, through unraveling truth and meaning, can compassion and regard evolve for every living creature. Because we all breathe the One Breath, how can we feel apart or think we are separate? We thrive in the breathing of our coexistence.

Microcosm: In Sufi Dance
As I lie in our cabin at the lake, I listen to the environment's voice. The multilayers of sounds, like fabrics in different tones of design, float in the air, each in its dance, yet all in connection, creating a swirling Sufi dance of electricity, light and color that we, in our breathing, are one with.

is you, is me

We are the skin
of all peoples
The spirit of all animals, birds
trees, plants and flowers

We are the earth itself
walking about

The sun's morning eyes
The moon's casting glow
The ever changing mists
The life of the clouds

The waters of the sea
The dolphin's fin
There isn't anything
that isn't you or me

As a granule of sand
creates the beach;
every blade of grass, the meadow;
every current and tide, the seas

The heavens' rains of joy
The spring fragrance abound
Every sound, scent, feeling
Every pulse is the planet
is you, is me

"Soul-Tree Bathing"

CHAPTER 25

THE

BRAIN-TREE

We digest the consciousness of everything we ingest: the murdered cow, the slain bird, the news, our thoughts, belief systems, vitamins, pollution. Upon birth we incorporate the well-being as well as the self-abuse of those around us. If our bodies are irritated by pollutants, our behavior is also polluted. Nothing can be separated from its source or environment. We are our symptoms; they are our sub-personalities expressing themselves biologically. I question how enlightened we can be if our systems are disturbed.

I am increasingly conscious that we gain nutritional benefit from the digestion of relevant philosophies as well as from the food we consume. Our living process, both biologically and spiritually, is in symbiosis with the Earth's. As with the rivers and streams, may the flow of our inner systems be clear, metabolizing the circulation of incessant change.

Today, while listening to Mozart's *The Magic Flute,* I drew a symbolic version of "The Brain-Tree." I had just finished reading Francis Jeffrey's thesis on the ecology of the brain and realized more extensively how to nurture my inner environment. I wish to fertilize the roots of my brain-forests with healthy, imaginative thoughts and perceptions rather than to allow pollution to invade my consciousness. I thrive in the nectar of imagination, the pollen of ecstasy, in union with the highest powers.

THE
I CHING:
27. I / THE CORNERS
OF THE MOUTH
(PROVIDING
NOURISHMENT)
This is an image of providing nourishment through movement and tranquillity. The superior man takes it as a pattern for the nourishment and cultivation of his character. Words are a movement going from within outward. Eating and drinking are movements from without inward. Both kinds of movement can be modified by tranquillity. For tranquillity keeps the words that come out of the mouth from exceeding proper measure, and keeps the food that goes into the mouth from exceeding its proper measure. Thus character is cultivated.

> We gain nutritional benefit from the digestion of relevant philosophies as well as from the food we consume.

~

My brain-tree can bask in this sweet air and let its seeds multiply into the eternal fruit of paradise.

Flexibility and resilience are essential if our brain-trees are to withstand the shocks of life. We must be rooted in our deepest and most fecund soil. We receive blessings from the gods, yet we must be ever vigilant to see through the pollution that disrupts our consciousness. Toxins make the fruit drop early; blossoms may die in the fumes. It is essential to remember not to put energy into the discordant, not to echo its abrasive sound. In using discrimination, we keep the predators out of our brain-garden.

May we offer our trees' branches infinite space to grow, and our buds the light of awareness so they may flower and bear fruit.

the timeless metabolized

Within my myriad hemispheres
an electric sea of filial threads
lures me to live,
the currents of brain-grasses swaying,

To explore the labyrinthian archives
of my mind;
The timeless aeons await

I, impassioned beyond patience,
eat temporal minutes without taste,
refuting skin as separation

Drawn to metabolize
the electron messages of seed,
the codes within my core

They have no urgency
in their timelessness
My every seed has lived
the two billion aeons:

The eternal instant beckons

But some threads are vines entangled,
mapping realities;
the keyless gates of illusion

Their shadows leave me
in yesterday's shade

I break the toughened tendrils
viewing innumerable keys, combinations—

The timeless metabolized;
The union of all times

"Haven at Julia's"

HOLOGRAPHIC

HEALTH

Philosopher Alfred North Whitehead speaks about life appearing as a compilation of fragmentary experiences. Our lives truly consist of innumerable neuronic interconnections. We are who we are because of what we are — biologically, spiritually, mentally and emotionally. By understanding our multidimensionality we better understand our health. Although we are captives of our genetic seed, our biology and consciousness are one and we may "trimtab"* toward our highest potential.

The taint of unloving feelings can act like gravity upon the gossamer of ascendance. Toxic feelings travel through the body and manifest as countless inflammations and diseases. Physical pain that manifests in the body as disease can not be distinguished from the emotional trauma we have experienced and absorbed. Molecular memories are recorded and, as tapes, replay in our bodies.

Memes of toxic emotions can be contagious, manifesting as disease. Anxiety, for example, is like a plague whose memes are spread from one person to another. It is the disease-fuel of our times, emitting static, producing escalating health problems. Fear is also spread like an illness. However, our awareness can resist infectious thought, protecting our immune systems. A healthy mind keeps our mental ecology free of fear and its endless symptomatology. Our consciousness offers flexibility to our immune system.

* see glossary

Our
consciousness
offers flexibility
to our immune
system.

To maintain a healthy mental and emotional ecology, let us observe our symptoms. They are our wise friends, asking us to give up what is not vital for our being. Our body is demanding that we acknowledge its biological reality. The biological symptom speaks to liberate the spirit of its injury and to understand its physical truth. If we recognize its message, we may learn to heal ourselves.

Yet, we have been conditioned and intimidated by the one-dimensional "cures" of the medical profession that undermine our power for self-healing. We are advised to follow procedures rather than to do our own research, exploring a holographic range of possibilities.

Life is a continual process of regeneration and integration, our awareness being our most essential preventative medicine. May we treat health issues with underlying faith in our inner physician.

with uncontrived heart

The rustling voices
Of dried leaves
Write their songs
On the evening breeze

Gestures of
twilight trees beckon

We walk upon their root
Upon the storm-fed earth
Upon the ashes of the fire
That burnt their bark

Can we ask for more
Than to grow with them
As one of them?

To feed as they
On the ash of yesterday

To grow the mutant flower
Only fire can birth

Ah, yes
To grow as a tree
With uncontrived heart

"Angels, Wards, Shadows"

CHAPTER 27

PARADOX IN PARADISE: THE COEXISTENCE OF OPPOSITES

Lately, I've been pondering some opposite yet complementary forces: male and female, light and dark, birth and death. In the pendulum's movement, both sides are inherent. Opposites are dynamic interplayers essential to evolution. The tension required to keep our seesaw in suspension, in balance between these opposite forces, is the tension that can enable or cripple our lives.

I observe that people externalize their anxiety, desperation, manifesting their human condition in wars and disease. The imbalance creates waste, crime and accidents. Opposite dynamics need not conflict; they may co-exist in the One Energy Wave requesting new channels of expression in the fusion of their complementary forms. Each force has its alchemical role. In this holograph of integration, opposite views may meld into creative expansion.

Life embodies opposites. In the miracle of birth is the possibility of death. A blessing carries its curse.

THE I CHING: 38. K'UEI / OPPOSITION

In general, opposition appears as an obstruction, but when it represents polarity within a comprehensive whole, it has also its useful and important functions. The oppositions of heaven and earth, spirit and nature, man and woman, when reconciled, bring about the creation and reproduction of life. In the world of visible things, the principle of opposites makes possible the differentiation by categories through which order is brought into the world.

> When we
> transcend our
> conflicts, our
> dualities within,
> we can under-
> stand that in our
> diversity is our
> reconciliation.

Within the "yes" may be "no." The struggle for survival is inherent in our very existence. We are all living in a jungle, whether we live in the wilderness or the city. Innumerable types of predators exist with their varying politics; ones that steal the psyche, others that attack the body. In one way or another, we are part of the cosmic food chain, in an incessant digestive process. Our diverse appetites consume and digest others' energy and ideas. We are all predators, interconnected by our need to survive. Life exists in tenuous balance, however vital or powerful it appears; we are bound to feel our vulnerability. In this philosophic prism, endless realities and their contradictions are reflected. No wonder desperation is innate in life. Yet, it takes the frost of winter to blossom the fruit.

We are still a primitive species; our consciousness is yet to be fully acquainted with the more transparent realms. We stay enclosed in the gravity of limited perception. Instead of succumbing to the way of thinking that creates alienation, let us be aware that we are of each other. Creative life-energy comes from the sustained tension of our differences, and the manner in which we balance these forces.

When we transcend our conflicts, our dualities within, we can understand that in our diversity is our reconciliation. The more we recognize our complementary diversity, the more unity will prevail.

Microcosm: Strange New Climate
A calmness, like a strange new climate pervades me by evening. It's the light after the dark, the understandings thrashed out of conflicts, the illumination of the greater perspective. Or, it's the calm of total weariness and the giving up into life.

in our hearts' love

to Thunder, our lion-dog (1983-1995)

Within the bliss of paradise
  lives the torment of hell

Within the life of every birth
  lives the force of death

Within the love of the lover
  lives the chance of hate

Within the bloom of fragrant rose
  lives the stench of rot

Within the summer's heat
  lives the winter's frost

Within the measurement of time
  lives the eternal

Within our present form
  lives the seed of our next

In our hearts' love for you,
  dying creature, you live forever

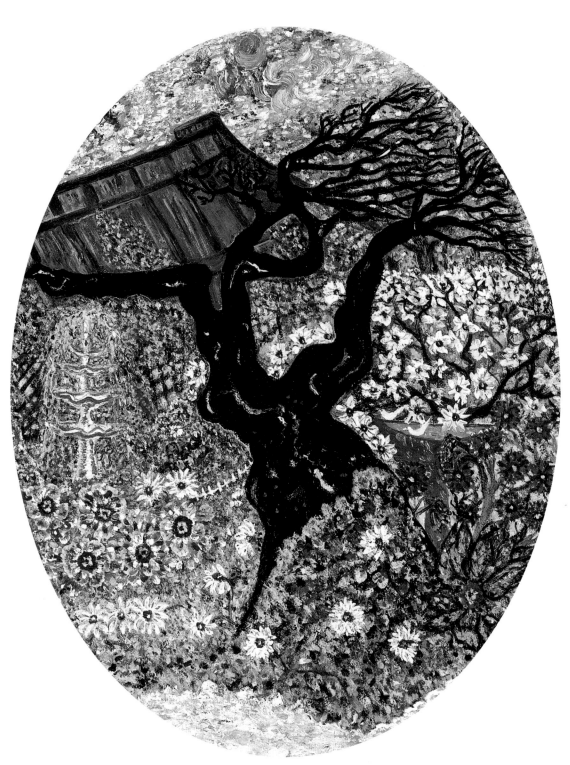

"Dead Tree at Pankosmion" *

* see glossary

MORTALITY / IMMORTALITY

As immortal beings, we are eternal gardens, reborn in myriad form. Consider the progression of the rose's bud to its full-petalled blossom; its fading fruits the seed of tomorrow. My philosophy mirrors the flower's life. I identify with Nature's mysteries rather than with the fear that feeds the predatorial approach toward aging.

If we appreciate the magnificent elephant with its wrinkles and sagging hide, we can see ourselves beyond the limit of human stereotype. When we detusk our elephants, we detusk ourselves. We allow our ivory to be stolen by the money-hungry predators who brainwash and terrify us about aging. We become victims of consumerism. I find my answers in the mirrored lake, in the silent voice of Nature, in the music of her climates, the deeper inner knowings. The meaning lives beyond the grasp, beyond exterior appearance, in the underpinnings of existence.

My roots dig deep as those of great trees, while my crown seeks greater heights. Although my bodily existence is temporal, within me is the grace of the ancient oak with its emerald spires.

Life dies only in its particular earth-garment. Concept binds us to its grasp. How can we thrive from mere categories when we are ceaseless fountains of the earth?

THE
I CHING:
[FROM 50. TING /
THE CALDRON]
All that is visible must grow beyond itself, extend into the realm of the invisible. Thereby it receives its true consecration and clarity and takes firm root in the cosmic order.

TAROT:
XIII DEATH
Death means parting, the great letting go, the end. It then also prepares the way for the new, for that which is to come.... The eternal embellishers, who do not understand it, read the card only to be the proclamation of something new and want to deny us the deep experience of parting, and the related life-accepting experiences.

In our continuous dying, in our detachment, fear is transformed, yielding to wisdom.

When our biology is no longer useful, when our work-love is over, why would we want to keep wearing the same outfit for the next performance?

At Andrew Molera State Park, I walk through the burial grounds of the cut-down eucalyptus. In testimony to eternal life, emerald growth sprouts from "dead" trunks. We also manifest our deaths endlessly in new forms. How can we, as walking trees, be anything but splendorous if our love pulses in affirmation of Nature as our own? Why should we be prey to the predators of fear and vanity?

All beginnings take the past and present into their next alchemical stage. Life and death exist within us simultaneously, breathing the same breath. New worlds are born as we inhale; old worlds die as we exhale. In living each moment as if it were the last, we create our afterlife, simultaneously integrating the past and the future as the present.

We are both constructive and destructive to ourselves as we refine ourselves through abrasion. "We channel our own demise," said Benjamin DeCasseres.

In the tidal change of the sand's patterns, I realize the gradual momentum necessary to make even the smallest change. Just as the tree whose fruit has fallen, just as the butterfly who discards its cocoon, the seasons carry our bodies through eternal climes of change.

The sunset gilds the aging pine wood of the cabin with a copper luminescence. The grasses with their empty husks give up their grain to another time. The dark edge of death's temporary finality consumes in silence the ending bloom. Death holds an invisible grasp on life's evanescent hand. The living and the dying wed in dialogue, a marriage of expansion and deterioration.

The unceasing manifests in the evolving kaleidoscope of eternity. Why be concerned about our dying? When we see the gardens in their endless seasons, may we so offer ourselves, yielding to such grace. For all we know our living is really our dying, and with our dying comes life.

Microcosm: William Melamed

A dear friend, lover and catalyst of poetic passion has been in the hospital dying of brain cancer. He was always tormented, filled with the passions of his Russian soul, trapped in the material realms. Yesterday at 5:30 a.m., I awoke consumed by a boiling fever. The heat was close to intolerable. I found out today that Bill had had a high temperature and had died at that time. I remember the love-connection that transcends distance. I feel his spirit's touch now as I write about him.

Experience brings wisdom to the aging in the riches their storms bestow.

song to my dying love
for William Melamed (1935-1991)

Breathe, my dearest man,
Breathe into the candle's light
Let your being drift
Into the River's currents

Let yourself be that current
Let yourself go to current
Be the symphony of
Your greatest dreams
My darling man

Perhaps it is I
Who is dying
In your leaving,
Not you, who is
Entering a new life

> The meaning lives beyond the grasp, beyond exterior appearance, in the underpinnings of existence.

≈

Microcosm: "Pops"

In his recent encounter with death, my father has metamorphosed. In his cocoon-like state, he now inhabits the realm between worlds. At last we meet between the seams. With his new biology comes a different philosophical state. In his neutral space of nonattachment, I feel closer than ever to him.

It saddens me to see this old elephant, this dignified animal barely able to walk. I tell him how proud I am of his strength. I tell him he is the strongest man in the world as he sits incapable of getting up without help. I tell him he is getting stronger every minute. I am speaking of the strength needed to endure his recent skirting with death on New Year's Eve. He has lived through another dying and is strong, in his weakness. How strange the vast contradictions. They express themselves in enigmas. Great nobility emanates from my ninety-one-year-old father as he overcomes his suffering with few words. He has been through so much in his recent years of hospitalizations, yet his dignity is firmly planted in his weakened tree.

My father's physical debilitation births fresh insights. Experience brings wisdom to the aging in the riches their storms bestow. Surely wisdom arises from the glowing ashes of a near-death experience. For Pops, in his weakness, every day was a near-death experience. In our continual dying, in our detachment, fear is transformed, yielding to wisdom. As we let go of attachment, our spiritual philosophy provides the bridge for transition to other worlds.

In his last stages, I'm not sure Pops recognizes me. I pour my love into him as an extension of myself, noticing his subtle response. Does it make a difference if he knows me? All that matters is the love I give him. Sometimes I weep at the approaching earthly loss of him; other times I accept his metamorphosis. I promise him our spirits will always be together, regardless of the form. I ask him to keep in contact with me on his voyage. And so I comfort myself about my father and his leaving this world as we know it.

As we let go of attachment, our spiritual philosophy provides the bridge for transition to other worlds.

eternal autonomy

I become friends
With the death
That lives within
No longer blaming others
For the moonless nights, sunless days

The world at large
Has its share of worms

And the white horse
Flies in darkness

The fears that sport
That tease and taunt
Are hairs of death's great skull
Once tamed and braided
They guide one up the hill

Then fear becomes
Our forgotten enemy
And death the friend of life
Giving it what it can't give itself
                    Eternal autonomy

When we see the gardens in their endless seasons, may we so offer ourselves, yielding to such grace.

"Neptune's Eve"

CHAPTER 29

PREJUDICE

AND

JUDGMENT

Prejudice and judgment arise from our denial of the shadow side of ourselves. Within us exists every force and wild creature. In ripping apart our cages of prejudice, we see through to the beast that lurks within. When we recognize the full spectrum of ourselves, we have no one to turn against; we cease using others as our scapegoat. Before we blame others or indulge in our so-called rational alibis, perhaps we should ask if the enemy is our own shadow, or separate.

Prejudice and judgment are the disease-fuel of our times, hovering over us like smog, a pollution to the senses, to the heart, to life. They reflect our mind's conditioning, blocking our inherent kingdoms within. If we abuse others through bias, we abuse ourselves. The petty mind shuts out the humanity of others, of ourselves and obscures the grandeur of the vaster spheres. The cowardly, the defensive, seeks bias over union.

Microcosm: The Projections We Cast on Others Come From Our Beasts Within

Through a revelation, I was able to purge many falsehoods. I saw deeply into my behaviors, my hypocrisies, my beasts

THE I CHING: 18. KU / WORK ON WHAT HAS BEEN SPOILED (DECAY)

When the wind blows low on the mountain, it is thrown back and spoils the vegetation. This contains a challenge to improvement. It is the same with debasing attitudes and fashions; they corrupt human society.

TAROT: XX JUDGMENT

This card...shows the decisive step to becoming oneself, the successful process of alchemical transformation from which something higher is created from a base substance.... The card can further stand for experiences in which we thankfully recognize that we have been freed from former entanglements, constraints, or fixed ideas.... it shows an awakening consciousness aroused from the narcotic blindness of existence and, in a bright moment, becoming aware of the unending freedom and greatness of creation.

Prejudice and judgment arise from our denial of the shadow side of ourselves.

within, weeping at the suffering I may have caused. I was shocked to see the truth of my behavior, the paradox and contradictions of my humanness. I realized that if I couldn't accept myself, I would project this bias onto others, blaming and judging them. To heal is to love fully, to be whole, to give my best to myself and others, to be in a perpetual practice of preventative medicine.

I forgive myself and others for their beasts within, understanding that when we feel an aversion, a strong loathing or wrath, it may be the very element we despise and need to acknowledge and heal in ourselves.

wiser for the view

To observe
the spectacle
of self
can be
bizarre,
comforting
ludicrous
or
whatever

Drop judgment
Add observation
That comprehension
makes one
wiser for
the view

"Dark Profile"

CHAPTER 30

BLAME

What is blame except being lame; it is our self-violation projected onto another. Blame stems from an intolerance of our own limits. How much of our interaction is projective, illusory? Let us juggle our power from balance, not bias.

As neuro-scientist Dr. John Lilly states, our minds are bio-computers generating our memory data. As fountains of Nature's forces, we have full power to choose the perceptions that best create our ideals. Blame and prejudice only produce self-made movies of violation. Out of boredom, our minds drive us to such indiscriminate distraction.

When we acknowledge that we can not blame another for our own limitations, we will realize that the path of personal responsibility is the path of liberation from the corrupt politics of our psychic and social enslavement. When we are aware of our projections, we become less critical of ourselves and others, valuing our interactions and each individual as a vital component of the Whole. A sum is only as whole as its parts. A civilization is only as healthy as its every individual.

I will no longer judge others from the intolerance of my own limitations.

Microcosm: The World as a Gymnasium

I have just felt alienation from more than one "friend." I've decided not to take it personally by feeling victimized. I see the world as a gymnasium where we all are defining who we are through others, and through what we do.

THE I CHING: [FROM 39. CHIEN / OBSTRUCTION]

Difficulties and obstructions throw a man back upon himself. While the inferior man seeks to put the blame on other persons, bewailing his fate, the superior man seeks the error within himself, and through this introspection the external obstacle becomes for him an occasion for inner enrichment and education.

TAROT: XV THE DEVIL

On the level of consciousness this card shows that we are becoming acquainted with our dark sides…. It can also — when lived in a completely uncritical manner — express a vision of the world in which we are afraid of the evil "out there" without understanding that we are only looking into the mirror of our own souls in doing so.

What is blame except being lame; it is our self-violation projected onto another.

I know that it is only in confrontation with ourselves and our wilderness that we really know ourselves. This requires listening to our alien voices, our unfamiliar thoughts and being enduringly patient and humane towards ourselves. I replace any blame I may hold with faith, the love that is greater.

i saw it in your face

I saw it in your face
And thought it was you
Not me, afflicted
And now I see and feel
It everywhere, the predators
The mouths ever ready

Why is there such hunger
With such abundance?
Why does the malaise
Hide its face?

Is it the blanched reality
Squeezed dry of illusion?
Is it the illness of our times
Poetry starved
Sensibilities robotized?

Is it living amongst the predatory
And feeling our vulnerability?

It may be a passing current
Played out in our ghosts

Hopefully moving on —
Letting the vacancy fill again

"Horse in Anguish Holds the Branch of Life and Death Between its Teeth"

SUFFERING

When we resist change, we suffer. Discomfort may be a symptom that we are inhibiting transition, are out of balance. Yet, when the thorns bleed the intimate chambers, change is forced into being. Death is inherent in the birth of every beginning.

In our suffering, our compassion increases, enabling us to be more empathetic. In our empathy for each other, we heal ourselves.

Suffering provides abrasion for refinement. Survival forces us to change; without the struggle and rawness, how would we evolve? These extremes are accelerating, forcing us through the bottleneck of critical transformation.

When I seek relief from earthly suffering, I remind myself of the need for a universal perspective. I remember not to resist pain, but to let it move through me like a wave. Life is a refining process through which we are sculpted by the winds and storms.

I feel more circuited than ever to the higher resonance, to the golden vibrations. The pain and struggle that are part of my odyssey have taught me a comprehension of the earthly, of myself so that when faced with a challenge, I often have the capacity to rest outside of the complexity. Only in simplicity can complexity coexist in harmony.

The oracle's voices speak through me and I receive the guidance that I request. All the assistance I need offers itself.

THE I CHING: 21. SHIH HO / BITING THROUGH

This hexagram represents an open mouth with an obstruction between the teeth. As a result the lips cannot meet. To bring them together one must bite energetically through the obstacle.

TAROT: 5 OF CUPS

The 5 of cups is the card of distress, sorrow and melancholy. It shows something broken that had been important to us up to now. It also says that we are not left alone with our pain...In any case, it shows that there is a solution. It calls upon us not to stay in this dismal state any longer than necessary.

Suffering provides abrasion for refinement.

~

Microcosm: In Paradise the Wounded Give Birth First
Sophia, the lovebird, cannot fly, but was the first to give birth in our aviary. In the wilds she would not have survived, much less given birth. In an environment of safety, handicap gives way to possibility. I realize this is true in my own life. The abrasive demands of existence continue to challenge, threaten my deeper, calmer connection, yet these challenges become rungs on the ladder to self-knowledge.

letting go

I let go
of pain
The abortions
of existence
The smoldering blaze
of self-incineration
The indigestion of
memories rehashed

Today, wildflowers sprout
from green meadows
of cleansed heart
amidst the emerald woodland

"Absorption"

CHAPTER 32

SELF-TYRANNY

THE I CHING: 59. HUAN / DISPERSION

Wind blowing over water disperses it, dissolving it into foam and mist. This suggests that when a man's vital energy is dammed up within him...gentleness serves to break up and dissolve the blockage.

At times, I feel enslaved by the government of my mind. I tyrannize myself with endless tasks. Sometimes, when I am most fragile, I am the least kind to myself. The primitive animal within, driven by its own need to survive, preys on my vulnerabilities. I am both tyrant and slave, playing my own cat-and-mouse games, capturing myself within self-made traps.

Sometimes the suffering that reverberates within is the effect of self-betrayal. In desperation, we may deceive ourselves, then repeatedly try to justify our compromise. We betray ourselves in every act of abuse. We become the victims and vultures of our fears, preying on the decay fear leaves behind. Truth comes in accepting our essential natures, in realizing we express the myriad climates of Nature as ourselves. If we burn our inner grasses, our sacred gardens within, we will burn another.

When I find myself preparing armies of defensive thought, I declare the end of warring within myself, the right to exalted living, transcendence from conflict and duality.

How am I, after much struggle, able to reach the plateau that re-grants me my birthright? So few of us seem able to give back to ourselves our most sensitive self, to uphold the integrity of who we really are.

I declare the end of warring within myself, the right to exalted living, transcendence from conflict and duality.

Every step into the unfamiliar requires an alert flexibility, letting transition be the way of existence.

Only in the deeper comprehension of our process can light be born. That light is our candle of love, liberating us from self-tyranny, freeing the essence of life.

the unknown thrives

Pursued by the fever
of my humanity
I become prey
to myself

Trapped by
the mind's seductions
I gaze upward
from the storm-drenched forest
seeing unleashed spirits wander
the canvas of the grey continuum
footprints of giants
leaving no tracks in eternity

The unknown thrives in the invisible
as the seed in the storm,
the sunny days
and in all change

"Yes or No"

CHAPTER 33

AMBIVALENCE/

IMMOBILITY

Perhaps most of our problems stem from limited perceptions. When we are ambivalent, doubtful, the issues we are struggling with may be metaphors for other underlying dynamics. It may be a time to observe without further entanglement, rather than to respond. Indecisiveness may be appropriate as a place of suspension, while we await the answers of cosmic time. Ambivalence may be requesting that we *live* our answers.

To try to force a decision prematurely is like trying to be in love. Thinking we need to make a decision may be the problem to begin with. A decision that does not come of its own should be set aside until its natural ripening. When it is time to act, we are ignited, and intuition guides us. Otherwise our minds can produce unnecessary confusion and exhaustion; the fruition of a decision will be reaped in its time.

We search for causes for our hesitance, but it is as natural as a climate. Ambiguity may polarize an evolving tension, or ignite creativity. We have been taught that we should know what we want, but "To know," said Benjamin DeCasseres, "is the Primordial Heresy." Instead of accepting our theater of intellectual hypocrisies, may we relax in the unknowable.

THE
I CHING :
60. CHIEH /
LIMITATION
It's a good thing to hesitate so long as the time for action has not come, but no longer.

TAROT:
XII THE
HANGED MAN
The Hanged Man, superficially seen, means that we are stuck and in a dilemma. However, with more thorough consideration we can see that in the external immobility there is a forced repose, as well as the necessity and opportunity to achieve a transformed view of the world and change one's life.

Indecisiveness may be appropriate as a place of suspension, while we await the answers of cosmic time.

~

Everything is strung together intergalactically. Forces keep the Earth in suspension, in rotation, an expectancy that could be the balance ambivalence seeks.

In the understanding of how we construct dualities, we may dissolve and transcend them. Ambivalence, when treated as suspension, can be a balanced state, a neutral ground of receptivity accumulating awareness in inner containment. With patience and careful observation, the underlying dynamics may offer revelations and self-knowledge.

With this perspective, we can live comfortably in hesitancy. With this crest-of-wave living, we surf the effervescence of yet another profile of expression. Ambivalence may be regarded as a characteristic of chaos and a catalyst for pending transition, providing momentum for our somersaults on the cosmic trampoline. According to contemporary Chaos Theory, chaos is not disorder but order that has yet to be decoded. Thus we may relate to ambivalence as suspended clarity. As Krishnamurti said, "Doubt is a precious ointment; though it burns, it shall heal greatly."

Microcosm: The Iron Egg
As a wave of melancholy surges through me, catching me up in a cloud of immobility, I see through its dynamics to the source. Indifference removes the iron egg of it laid upon my chest. Trying to act from my mind brings immobility. I lie down and let a cooling gust breathe through me. How soothing to feel its flow.

in doubt

For the bride who marries
In Doubt
When she says, "Yes"
She also says, "No"
Her selves so divorced
Can't marry

For the bride who marries
In Doubt
Wears an uncleanable gown
Its cumbersome train gathers dust
As she glances to view
Where she's been

Her hesitant veils never lift
Permanently draped
From the wind

For the bride who marries
In Doubt
Wears gloves which reach out to hello
As permanently part of her skin

For the bride who marries
In Doubt
When she says, "Yes"
She also says, "No"

A perennial bride, yet
Long married, to
Her persistent suitor...
　　　　　　　　Doubt

·

"Arm in the World"

CHAPTER 34

COMPETITION

THE
I CHING:
10. LÜ / TREADING
Heaven and the lake show a difference of elevation that inheres in the natures of the two, hence no envy arises. Among mankind also there are necessarily differences of elevation; it is impossible to bring about universal equality.... if inner worth forms the criterion of external rank, people acquiesce and order reigns society.

To try to outdo another is as senseless as being in competition with oneself. Comparing our capacities with others', or trying to outdo others for our own sense of importance, is self-defeating, although we may appear to win. Another rival always exists in this no-win game. The tyrant is owned by his slave. Because each wants power over the other, both become powerless.

Like most of society's programs, competition originates in survival instincts and is played out in the mind games we have accepted. How absurd the tyranny of competition, yet it is innate. Competition not only divides us within ourselves, but also produces insatiable drives. We externalize our rivals from our formidable foes within. We cannot have peace when we harbor our own competitive politics.

I realize that most recreational games are competitive by nature. I am not particularly referring to that issue but rather to the psychic hazards competition arouses.

In recognizing we are each essential in our own way, that no one is superior or inferior, harmony replaces rivalry.

Microcosm: The Bigger-Beak Mentality
Nereus, our male lovebird with the largest beak, has been monopolizing four of the six birdhouses in our aviary. When the birds have houses, they fight for their territory, although in our aviary, there are enough houses for all the lovebirds. Instinct takes precedence over conditioned reality.

We externalize
our rivals from
our formidable
foes within.

Since our beginnings, human nature hasn't changed much. Basic survival instincts still run our world, with the most aggressive taking control. Must we evolve biologically to move to the Sixth Dimension?

I can't help but think about how in our own lives, when survival instincts preside, the larger beak takes over. Perhaps my dream of people evolving is just a need for optimism. How do one's ideals fit into a world of competitive beaks? I don't have the answer except to say that our planet was bountiful and could be again if we transform ourselves beyond the "competitive beak" mentality. May we architect our ideals from the unity underlying diversity, apart from the disruption of competition. As our consciousness evolves, so does our biology. When united, each person's strength benefits all.

from life's otherwise
flood of domination

For the mind thrashing
Within conflict's grasp
Death thought-duels may offer sport
Ambivalent fencing to indulge

If this sport plays us
Muscling a shadow mountainous —
Beyond ascent
Its sword crucifies any freedom
Ripping our passport to nascent land

If this sport joins dawn's breath,
Inhabiting one;
The raven's beak pecks...
Autonomous decisions are in precision made

If six fingers of courage hold one's sword
This sport may offer transitory freedom,
A releasing —
From life's otherwise flood of domination

"Face of Suppressed Storm"

CHAPTER 35

DESCENDING

SPIRALS

THE
I CHING:
29. K'AN / THE
ABYSMAL
In man's world K'an represents the heart, the soul locked up within the body, the principle of light enclosed in the dark.

TAROT:
XVIII THE MOON
The Moon card leads us into the mysterious realm of darkness and night; into the image world of the soul.... It is the terror we feel when we walk through a deserted forest at night, although we don't think twice about crossing it during the day. It teaches us the nature of fear in the dark.... It is a journey into the depths....

As Tolstoy said, "Although I have everything in the world, I feel a sense of death." After all-consuming thrusts of energy, I find myself emptied, an opaque pool that can't reflect the heaven it once beheld.

I feel as if I have learned nothing as I reflect on the absurdity of my self-created circus, my grasps to ascend from the earthly plane, my vain attempts to convince Nature I am beyond suffering.

Because all is an illusion, I thought I could orchestrate joy, poetry — that in her endless gifts Nature was on my side. Now in her autonomy and indifference to my philosophic recipes, Nature has left me a hapless creature without wings. Without my energy I lose the capacity to create my world. It becomes dull and flat, lost from its former dimensions. My lover's handsome profile affects a feeling of loss rather than joy.

I am reminded that we are born alone and go out alone. I am in touch with that sovereignty as I walk our dirt road in the early morning moonlight. Feeling like an empty husk, I bend low to the ground, severed from my imagination. I have fallen from my heaven, my love-realm, with muddy wings, barely remembering the metabolism of Paradise.

Perhaps in grasping to explain life's meaning, we dissipate its pulse.

〜

I think Nature is indifferent to our explanations of existence. I, who try to outsmart death with visions of transcendence and humor, have only outsmarted myself.

Who rebels against the worm? I, an anarchist even to Nature's rules, am slain. Here, in a vacuum of futile weariness, I still will not succumb to misery's sobriety. At least I have my sense of the ludicrous, the absurd, without the need to justify.

Does Nature, in its solemn cycles and revolving alchemy, have a sense of humor? Nature, being ironic, has the wild humor born of the Cosmic Eye. As Dr. Timothy Leary once said, "If it's true, it has to be funny."

Perhaps in grasping to explain life's meaning, we dissipate its pulse. Perhaps if our need for justification of being were thrust aside, we would have more space for less constructed living. If we could only let the winds blow the ripples of our pools, let the images reform without endless interference by the industry of being human and be less in the mind, our true work-play may emerge.

Burning passions, desires and ambition eventually lead us to a need for restoration. In the balance between life and death lives an ennobling tension.

When we view the sometimes abrasive technologies of existence as hexagrams of transition, they are easier to accept. Through this comprehending, we can navigate away from fragmented reality, assuming an observer's pose. Liberated to the realms where suffering has no life, we experience the eternal.

Microcosm: Awaiting Possibility
I realize that the reason I haven't been able to be on vacation is that my mind has been tormenting me. Every decision I have made now lifts its ghoulish,

unshapen face and demands recrimination. The "nest" has been overcast with fog, providing little visual stimulation. To really behold Nature will require a complete release of the present haunting thoughts of an echoing isolation. How does one elevate oneself to a place where everything falls into a mosaic of meaningful design?

Now, as the great white clouds pass over the moon's face, a few hours before dawn, I sit looking out over the platinum sheen of undulating tides. I know that nothing essential can be received from the superficiality of the mind's contortions. I have decided that all I can do, in this exhaustive sense of futility, is not to will anything and just let whatever is, be.

In the balance between life and death lives an ennobling tension.

dawn's cocoon

Severed from my wings
I am mortal again

I taste the subliminal poisons
Of annihilated seed
The congestion of feelings
The dam of stagnant streams

I purge my night-wail
Into the ebony surge
The infinite seas below

And wait in the echo
Of a shallow silence

In the mud of temporal time
Where Eternity has vanished

In a sodden humility
I am enshrouded
I am there
In dawn's cocoon

Yet another tree
After the storm

Nature, being
ironic, has the
wild humor
born of the
Cosmic Eye.

"Glaciers of Antarctica"

THE

ISOLATION

GRIP

Isolation may originate from being divided against oneself. In this cold division within, we are torn from our roots as if exiled from our own country. We feel alone, even in a crowd, because we have lost our integration, our innate power. If we attempt to heal the split by following our restless desires, we pave a futile path. Lament is unanswered by worldly seductions. Would I betray my soul in the ache of loneliness, thus rewounding the origin of my pain?

A panic and desperation may arise when we sense we are captive to the world's systems, as well as to the fragility of our own nervous systems. We may feel trapped, like birds in cages. When our functioning is limited, threatened, we can feel imprisoned within ourselves, at the mercy of life, its ruthless irony.

We live the alone, then travel to the Alone, yet we are never really alone. In the consistent contradictions of life, the oneness underlying multiplicity is omnipresent and accessible. Our song, whether harmonious or dissonant, echoes throughout the hologram of existence.

THE
I CHING:
[FROM 24. FU /
RETURN]
Walking in the midst of others, one returns alone.

TAROT:
4 OF SWORDS
In the scope of our personal relationships this card shows that we are isolated. We either feel ourselves to be deserted and locked out of the great game of love, or we are lonely and careworn within a relationship. With this background, the 4 of Swords is a warning that we are on the best path to relinquishing and resigning. We should now allow ourselves peace and quiet…. If we ignore the warning of this card and continue to torture ourselves, it can easily lead to the depths of despair.

Isolation may originate from being divided against oneself.

Microcosm: Seared Heart

Last night I was gripped by the deep isolation that comes from living in a world that never seems kindred. I felt set apart except for my love and deep compassion for humanity.

Because I am caught in yesterday's suffering, struggling for clarity, the splendors of today are stifled. My lover and I are out of harmony, communication muffled by an underlying anger. It is very cold, raining and windy. I wrestle to be free of a lurking violence, to let go, to become once again the untroubled instrument.

to be human

There, in the crashing darkness
without another eye to behold
There, in violent splendor,
a haunted loneliness stumbles on

An alien creature,
lost from its species,
eyes discomforted by human glance,
body sodden with pores of isolation
grasps beyond the storms,
beyond the turbulent tides below

To reconcile
the primal savagery,
the mute terror
of what it means
to be human

"Marine Profiles"

CHAPTER 37

SOLITUDE /

SOCIABILITY

One may have to bear endless isolation to create the space to realize one's essential nature. As Rilke, Thoreau and other writers and artists have said, solitude is a prerequisite to self-discovery. We may cultivate our inner worlds by giving ourselves seclusion in time and space.

Invention requires an uninterrupted environment, both internally and externally. Sometimes the isolation that comes from being lost to exploration is like that of a deep-sea diver needing to resurface to reconnect to earthly reality.

Sometimes our work requires isolation. Although we are all inextricably connected, a sense of alienation may come from being required to work apart in a solitary and refined environment.

As Van Gogh wrote in a letter to his brother Theo from Saint-Remy, "*Life is short and time passes quickly. If one is master of one thing and understands one thing well, one has at the same time insight into and understanding of many things…. Whoever would prefer to be quietly alone with his work and who wants but very few friends will go safest through the world and among people…. One must never let the fire go out in one's soul, but keep it burning.*"

The mystical requires hermetic containment, chemistry for the germination of creation.

THE
I CHING:
[FROM 3. CHUN /
DIFFICULTY AT THE
BEGINNING]
In order to find one's place in the infinity of being, one must be able both to separate and to unite.

TAROT:
IX THE HERMIT /
4 OF WANDS
The Hermit is the card of seclusion and turning within…. We find repose and, above all, are separate from bustling activity and crowds of people.

The 4 of Wands shows a phase of peacefulness in which we…come out of our shell in order to enjoy life…. This means…an increased joy of living, as well as an inner process of opening up, through which we directly take part in the life around us and experience a deep solidarity in our contacts with other people.

The mystical requires hermetic containment, chemistry for the germination of creation.

~

Microcosm: A Wild and Endangered Species

A sign at my first wilderness home read, in Portuguese, "Solitude without loneliness." Now I more fully understand the meaning: The more I become one with the Divine, the less loneliness there is in solitude.

I empathize with Sophia, the lovebird, who, although she cannot fly, does not feel sorry for herself. She can not live like the others; neither can I. My instrument of being demands great solitude to unfold its process, its art. Yet my interest in people draws me into a diversity of inspiring and collaborative friendships.

Solitude and interaction are equally essential, having their own rhythms in varying cycles. Time and distance from my art and other devotions are required for me to experience a more expansive orientation. My rhythms and cycles dance between the internal and external worlds.

compassion for the sad

There in the wilderness
Upon the mountain top
I leave my loneliness,
My creature's hide

I leave my loneliness
Hung on a peg,
A discarded robe
Of spotted skin,
Freckles and habits

I leave it there alone, without me
As I stride the city,
See people, make acquaintances,
Love my lover, love my father
I become human
In another way, again

A steppen-creature,
Neither wolf nor woman,
Not lonely, not sad,
Not in this world,
Or the other,
Half human, half creature

Deserted loneliness
Leaves compassion for the sad

"Women Worry Over Wounded Warrior"

CHAPTER 38

MISSION / AMBITION: THE BUSINESS OF ART

One must not unresistingly let himself be swept along by unfavorable circumstances, nor permit his steadfastness to be shaken. He can avoid this by maintaining his inner light.... In some situations indeed a man must hide his light, in order to make his will prevail in spite of difficulties in his immediate environment.

TAROT:
V THE HEIROPHANT

The Heirophant represents the search for deeper meaning, fulfilling tasks, and a true calling. Furthermore, this card can also indicate individual situations where we are called upon to remain true to our moral principles in our business attitude and not let ourselves become entangled in shady deals.

With my unrestrainable urge to spawn my art into the world is also the need to be removed from the world as much as possible. How do we distinguish between mission and ambition, the desire to communicate and the pursuit of self-importance?

In order not to be an industrialized human, a robot, we must function apart from the corruptive systems as much as possible. This means keeping our integrity, our humanness intact.

Benjamin DeCasseres reminds us to let our ideals lead us in our pursuits, independent of consequence; the world may need what is least popular or acceptable.

Microcosm : The Gallery
My need to connect with humanity is deep. My desire to be invisible seeks its opposite in the visible. Although my art takes me to great beauty, seldom does inspiring

How do we distinguish between mission and ambition, the desire to communicate and the pursuit of self-importance?

interaction result. What about a gallery, I thought, in which I could make my world visible? Would the visibility that I yearn for be satisfied in this way?

In the past I have become temporarily corrupted by my dealings with the world's systems. I have become someone else in order to deal with the frustrations and complexities. I only become involved because of my aspiring urge to bring my expressions to the world, to communicate in a meaningful way. In so doing, I am being true to myself, genuine to what is meaningful to my core.

I did open a gallery and, one year later, am still disturbed by the busywork of commercialism. I am in a constant state of preparation and expectancy. If of the world, one must toil. I have turned myself inside out, in order to expose my art. I feel grotesque. What it takes to create the sacred can be quite different from what it takes to offer it. While striving to make my work available, I am losing the quality of living it took to create it. What once was my fragrant space is now polluted by the debris of endless deadlines and business decisions. In being a merchant, I feel coarse fibers disrupting my more refined weaving. Being an executive in the business world is not for me; the only way I can author my essence is to be free from the results of its expression.

So, I feel the conflict between my aesthetics and the world's. Appalled by the hypocrisy of the art market, I realize I do not want to support its destructive systems. How could my art-seeds thrive in such a wasteland? My plans appear limited and self-coercing compared to the *sublime in undesign*. As poet Rainer Maria Rilke said, "You must live your answers." So I am reminded to be willed to the gods as an exploring diver of the unconscious, resurfacing with its gems as my discoveries.

Ideas create much labor; I am both the chosen and the slave.

In the end, I closed the gallery. I intended instead to bathe in my creative moons rather than scorch in the suns of aspiration. With so much distraction, I had lost touch with my essential vision of art, art as a way of living and being, as intention itself. What could be a finer gift than to bring our unconditioned spirit to our work and friendships? What gift created in joy will not bring joy? The very quality I wanted to bring to the world had been drained from me.

The Greater Intelligence will provide the forces to disseminate my creations; the bridge we seek is already inherent in the seed, not a thing apart. As the wind blows the flower's seed, so will my art seminate; I do not need to will it. If the world calls my work forth, the forces will present the bridges, as the breeze to the seed. And if the present world has no need, that is also acceptable.

...the bridge we seek is already inherent in the seed, not a thing apart.

let me be

As I stalk
the smoldering moons within,
I plead for release
from the scorching suns
of aspiration

Let my poetry
be silence within,
mute as the dormant maple tree,
lavender in its winter bareness,
bearing no leaves of greeting
as I walk by

Let me be
the tree in rest,
the winter's pod
Just let me be

I plead for the urgings to relent
for my voice to be still,
not needing to be heard,
not needing to be seen
Let peace be mine

These whirling suns consume
in the chaos they bear
I know not what day it is
what anything is

I stumble upon my toes,
                falling up

Let our
ideals lead us
in our pursuits,
independent of
consequence.

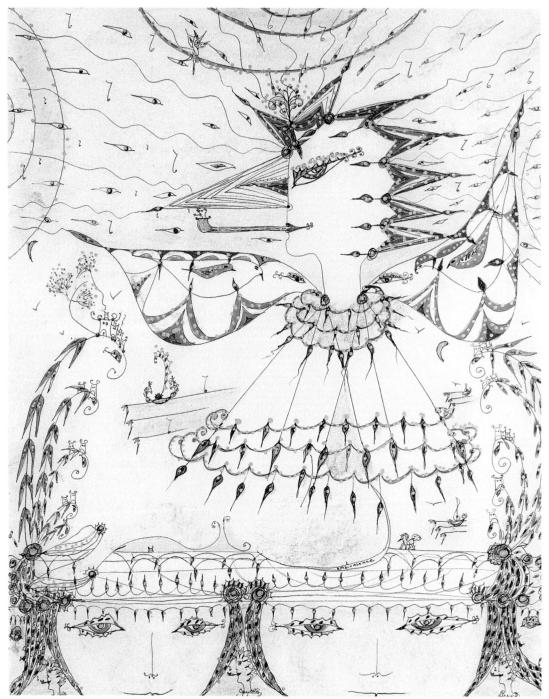

"Intuition and Rationality"

CHAPTER 39

FEELING /

THINKING

The merely conceptual divides the Whole, severing feeling from mind, producing imbalance, an isolating maze. Feelings are lost; the crown of the tree drifts without roots. Desiccated, we can no longer germinate. A rooted connection is essential to wholistic thinking.

Within somatic experience lies molecular knowledge; our whole being is engaged. All of us beholds, not just the eye. A synthesis allows an understanding through all our senses rather than through only one facet of the cerebral gymnasium.

From the aesthetics of acute sensibility, a certain intelligence emerges. It is the intelligence of honesty, the gentleness of understanding, the connection to the Earth, a pure and positive receptivity to all that Is. It is the recognition that comes in knowing our vast natures, the miracles we are, and in knowing that we can design our visions in our every thought. These sensitivities connect us to the Earth, to a more refined humanity.

Yet, what causes our overly specialized species to emphasize the analytic over other antennae? The purely cerebral blocks our ability to feel out of fear of losing control. Perhaps the exaggeration of our mental approach serves to counteract the extremes of our emotions. Many of our most accelerated drives come from fear and anxiety.

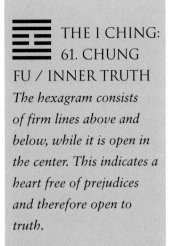

THE I CHING: 61. CHUNG FU / INNER TRUTH

The hexagram consists of firm lines above and below, while it is open in the center. This indicates a heart free of prejudices and therefore open to truth.

TAROT: KING OF CUPS

The King of Cups embodies...our search for transcendental experience...and the mysterious unification with the original source.... He has the knowledge that this area is closed forever to the intellectual approach and can only be experienced by those who open themselves to intuitive introspection and are prepared to let themselves be found and touched.

> The merely conceptual divides the Whole, severing feeling from mind, producing imbalance, an isolating maze.

To comprehend, however, we need a 360-degree perspective. The most direct path is intuition. As Krishnamurti said, "Intuition is the highest point of intelligence, and keeping alive that intelligence is inspiration." Intuition carries the gnostic message.

Feeling is our instrument for weaving our personal mythology throughout existence. Existence is a yielding, converging electronic wave; to feel its current, its will, is to let it take us. As energy channels suspended in space, may we trust and experiment in the interplay. Symbiosis is our most intimate process. When our minds are unfettered, our sensing is instinctual, intuitive and direct. When we yield to our sensibilities, the codes of existence are revealed.

I let my molecular sensings guide me. I know the difference between the rawness of what Dr. Timothy Leary termed survival emotions and the delicacy of cellular sensing.

I answer my life somatically, with every atom of my cellular being unified in my decisions. I will not strategize myself out of my own nature; that which is in accord directs me. In living the unconditioned, my senses are vibrant, inquiring and receptive, inviting the expanding intimate to reside within.

Microcosm: Testing for Intunement

I've finally agreed not to do anything that feels out of resonance, regardless of seductive illusions that may attempt to dissuade me.

I trust my organic being and its direct response. I can be the Tao of myself, and let go into the Greater, the Simpler. Every reality wave is somatically tested for intunement. This harmony is the song that propels, unfurling my life voyage.

sometimes i follow

The great passion
  breathes my soul
    spawns my wild seed

Is the ink of my pen
  colors of my palette
    blood pulsing my veins

Passion sweeps
  the brush strokes
    across eternity's face;
      I am but its tool

An instrument of song
  an exploratory experiment
    in the unknown

Who am I
  to grasp control?

I ride the waves of time
  not knowing the shores
    I'll be swept upon

My mind attempts navigation;
  sometimes I follow

"The Robot Man and the Lovers"

CHAPTER 40

SENSITIVITY /

ANESTHESIA

In the hospital of the world, there is no asylum for the sane.

The terrorism, brutalities of our times exemplify our anesthetized sensibilities. Without our ideals, we have no self-reference. We stare blindly rather than behold. We metabolize the *industry* of living rather than the unconditioned life, giving up our sensitivities for robotic repetition, the nonexperience of the dulled. May we tune in with all of our antennae; in this receptivity we become vulnerable, capable of change.

Technology is a key to transforming our communication and information systems, and to inhabiting space. Genetic engineering may lengthen our lives indefinitely and perhaps be an answer to our biological evolvement. But unless our inner garden is cultivated, robotics will replace our personal poetry with the void of technology, the abstraction without blood. Our technology will develop into a more organic whole only when we do. What we create is a mirror of our evolution, or, de-evolution.

As an endangered species, what vulnerable creatures we are in our interdependency and complexity. The compassion that made me, as a child, bury dead ants in matchboxes, erect crosses and sing hymns to dead hamsters, sometimes makes it difficult to be in harmony with the aggressive majority. In our calloused society,

TAROT:
2 OF SWORDS
True conviction can only occur when our perceptions are also carried on the level of our feelings. This area of the unconscious, portrayed by the ocean and the moon on the card, is cut off. The crossed swords, the limitations of the intellect, hinder admittance. The card thereby characterizes the difficult position that we fall into when we struggle for clarifying perception without listening to our inner voice.... The danger shown here lies in ultimately standing paralyzed in front of a pile of parts without knowing if we can create a new unity out of them. Without being able to approach the ocean, which represents the whole, we can only produce rationally-oriented partial perceptions that, although possibly brilliant, do not provide us with an inner peace.

> In our calloused society, sensitivity is not valued for its intelligence; yet genius does not exist without sensitivity.

~

sensitivity is not valued for its intelligence; yet genius does not exist without sensitivity.

I notice the rugged, the tough of our species adapt more readily to being defensive than do the sensitive. I remember Dr. Carl Jung's four personality types: feeling, thinking, intuitive and sensation. While sensation-types hunger for the stimuli of the city, the senses of the introvert recoil from its overload.

A safe environment reduces the need for survival response, providing possibilities for our healthiest creations, for our violin strings to be strummed by infinity. To tune my instrument of eternity with sensitivity, preserving it from corruption, is a full-time challenge.

As an artist I find it particularly essential to keep the strings of my instrument finely tuned, letting the tides of freedom bathe and replenish. Why expose the delicacy of our senses to pollution; our aesthetics rely on them. They are elixirs of ecstasy that need to be protected and encouraged to flourish. Those of us who possess these sensitivities remind me of the yellow canary used by the coal miners to test the quality of the air in the mines. Likewise, artists and other sensitives are the barometers of society.

Microcosm: Tracing the Origin
The beacons of boats in the bay below silhouette the spines of cypress trees. I am entranced when my mind can be free, as it is now. When I feel the contractions of abuse, I become aware of the discomfort, the invasion, and remind myself that the origin is often born in the burial of feeling, in the anesthetized.

the robot

man's in a trance
a slow death dance
    he's just
an inorganic tool
    covering
concrete guts to duel
    computerized
unlived lives
    in
self-made sterile hives
    gulping
instant numbered flab food
spit for the dummy's tube
    ebbing
blood drips each day
anesthetized away
    a zoo
of numb civilization
    with no
spiritual realization
    the robot
man's in a trance
a slow death dance

"*St. George and the Dragon*"

CHAPTER 41

MATERIALISM /

SPIRITUALITY

Insensitivity feeds false power, greed, manipulation. What is sought outside is to compensate for the lack inside. If power is intrinsic, to capture it outside is unneeded.

Our relationship to money provides a curious spectacle for a behavior study. The slavish need to acquire and consume is not based on actual need. The perception of need actually produces need, creating financial stress. We are employed by our desires. In reality, there could be plenty without the exploitive games that produce scarcity. By influencing us about what we should own or who we should be, the media condition us to believe we have needs, a "disorder" or "lack." Using endless disguises of exploitation, the media program these dependencies, imprinting them repeatedly.

As philosopher Alan Watts said in his 1968 seminar at Esalen Institute in Big Sur, "It's our imagination that believes the poverty." Imbalance breeds an insatiable appetite.

In Western culture, we value material possessions, what can be seen rather than the cultivation of our inner beings. One could protest there is much satisfaction in grand mansions, fast sport cars and whatever else expensive taste dictates, but in Beverly Hills, from the age of fifteen, I saw and experienced the shallow void of the superficial. Those who acquire financial excess are often tyrannized by their possessions, burdened by the endless maintenance

TAROT:
IV THE EMPEROR /
THE QUEEN OF CUPS
The Emperor represents the structure-giving element, our desire for stability, security and continuity.... He is the equivalent of our drive for civilization with which we build houses, heating and air conditioning systems to protect ourselves from heat, cold, and rain.... The Emperor points out our sense of order, sobriety, discipline, responsibility, and pragmatic conduct, as well as the exaggeration thereof....

The Queen of Cups... is the ruler of our unconscious powers of the soul...the clear-sighted interpreter of our dreams, and the prophetess who penetrates the fog.... The sources of her wisdom flow in secrecy and defy the grasp of scientific reason.

We are employed by our desires.

and accompanying anxieties. For example, many people in the luxurious ghetto of Beverly Hills live with panic buttons, alarm systems blinking, their swimming pools unused. With money as their God, they are ever in need of more. Is the exaggerated lust for money a panacea for whatever is missing?

With money as our honey, so we buzz, but what we procure may not be so sweet.

We become increasingly depersonalized and specialized in the accelerating complexity of economic demands. The poli-economic systems, parasitic and cannibalistic, program us to slave for our desires, crippling us with pressuring tensions that keep us locked in consumerism.

It is difficult for a person to be innovative in the existing systems. Our survival instincts cage us, imprisoning us on a primitive level of existence. Working endlessly, we pay the government taxes that may work against us. As we perpetrate such injustices, we become blind to our birthright.

Money can be handled with the same integrity as everything else. If treated in a dissociated way, the results are dissociated. We tend to treat money in the same way we treat ourselves. Those who exploit others also exploit themselves. Regardless of the amount of our finances, may our mind and spirit be integrated, guiding our actions, always considering the possible effect.

The way we *think* could make the difference. Perhaps evolution will sculpt more wisdom into our beings. Our answers to survival and prosperity lie in the multi-dimensional aspects of awareness, in the synthesis of science and the ideals of spirit. Poverty is bred from an imbalance of power emanating from the ruptured Spirit. We will have less impoverishment when we account for ourselves and our effect on every other living creature.

Microcosm #1: Growing up in Beverly Hills

I grew up in a world that put material values before the individual, before feeling. One's appearance, one's car, one's home were most important.

I was fifteen years old when my family decided to leave Santa Monica and move to Beverly Hills. Until then, the best part of my life had been riding my horse, Mable, a kindred spirit, in the rural area surrounding my home.

When we moved, this way of life was lost to the plastic and glitter of Beverly Hills. When friends visited, I was embarrassed by our house; some had never seen wall-to-wall carpeting in a bathroom. I felt uncomfortable because people tended to see the material world before the spiritual. When I was seen, it was as a business tycoon's daughter. No one saw into my soul. My family couldn't know me, nor could the society I inhabited.

After I moved to Beverly Hills, I had Mable put to sleep. She was old, wasn't well, wasn't eating, and therefore, I rationalized, couldn't survive going out to pasture. Although all this was true, I see now that what I did to Mable was what I was doing to myself, putting my own spirit to sleep along with hers. At school I separated from my unique friends and, instead, wanted to fit in with the exclusive *club* group. I suddenly was bereft from my alliance with life, having betrayed my own nature. As I remember Mable, I vow never to put my horse-spirit to sleep again.

Years later in Beverly Hills, my two daughters gave my life its primary purpose. The rest — the tennis competitions, the modeling, the movie contract offer, the acting workshops, the approval I received when living from my more superficial nature — reflected my experimentation and my attempt to adapt to convention. I was offered a simple way to get approval. Why didn't I take the path

Imbalance breeds an insatiable appetite.

Material success does not lessen the relentless striving or aspiration.

of easy gratification? My explorer nature proved to be stronger than these other stages. I had always been curious about what lay behind human fabrications. I was drawn to experience the unknown, the wilderness of my soul. But first I had to give up the old prescriptions, the illusion that society had more to offer. Since then I have distanced myself from society's systems, from the entropic mind programs designed to mechanize reproduction and fuel the techno-industrial economy.

Not having the nature required to be *in the world,* I have always been fatigued by public systems, schools and universities. I daydreamed and doodled my way through school, but was always fascinated by art and psychology. I found the subtler sensitivities of the natural world and its creatures more entrancing than academia. My spiritual survival was at stake no matter how comfortable my home. My imagination is my salvation; the world of ideas, my sport.

In my capacity for creation, I feel truly alive. The world of stereotypes, labels, trends is only interesting to study and observe. The static of the economic buzz disrupts my song. The mystic's root must be self-planted to be nourished in a world where cars and consumption rule, where one *is* one's car.

Microcosm #2: Liberated From Ambition
Here, in our aviary among the birds, trees and plants, I imbibe life's perfection. There, in the sterile environment of a hospital, lies my eighty-nine-year-old father, reduced to bare survival. How sad to see a man with a tyrant's will unable to walk or feed himself. In my Pops I see that in time we may become our opposites, that despite our accomplishments, in one sense biology holds the cards.

I had always thought the golden years would bring comfort, surrounding us with loved ones; reaping the benefits of our life's work. I hoped to be able to provide this for Pops.

I have thought that if we began our ascension, our path into the spiritual early in life, that by the time we reached our last years, we would find the transition to the next sphere a familiar path, simply a continuum.

Those who have lived only on the material level have not yet walked their garden path with their soul's feet. Their physical bodies depleted, their souls request to spin their gossamer ladders to further ascension.

My father was not driven by the spiritual to ascend the Earthly. His power and fulfillment came from outer accomplishment, from his financial genius. Now, with his disintegration, perhaps serenity will be his. He has been relieved of his extreme survival drives, commencing when he was growing up in an English ghetto during World War II, contending with air raids, bombs and the responsibility of being the father to his younger brothers and sister. Now Nature is easing him of the strife, struggles and wars he has endured. He is like an old animal.

Now that his aggressive drives have diminished, he is released from the enslaving hierarchies of the material world. His drives produced enormous work for him. Material success does not lessen the relentless striving or aspiration. Now, with the transformation born of age, my Pops can regrow the feathers that were clipped.

Another facet of my father is being revealed: Without his tyrannical drives and his conditioning, he is free to be loving. His dynamic and busy mind no longer works for the systems of the man-made world. Now, in his eleventh hour, his barest being is revealed to those who can travel with him to the in-between world he now inhabits. His memory, liberated from ambition's entrapments, no longer grasps the familiar as an orientation.

With money as our honey, so we buzz, but what we procure may not be so sweet.

The perception of need actually produces need, creating financial stress.

He grasps nothing and thus is freer than he was in his forceful, dynamic life. Time, in the last of his sunsets, has enlightened him; he is noble, braver than ever, as he stands without ego, naked, a leafless tree facing the climes. His nature has graced him to appear in such quiet, subtle splendor.

As we sit conversing in his living room, the last of the sun's rays touches his silent gray hairs. There, at the end of day, in his sunset, we are of the same light. The radiance is the feeling shared, the touching of hands, of souls, in our vulnerability. He is so dear, so fragile, yet his nature is ever strong in its drive to stay alive.

I tell him the story of his life, about the hundreds of thousands of houses he has built, of his great success. I say, "Isn't it amazing?" He says, "It's amazing." He remembers nothing. Does the leaf as it falls from its stem remember its other lives? Is it even important to remember? Our memories lie in the eternal cellular labyrinths. He has gone beyond the limits of localization into the vaster spheres, where life lives us.

Five years after my father made his largest business deal, he became what they label "senile." I still wonder if when he sold his business, he lost his life's orientation, and thus became prone to ensuing health problems.

I find it interesting that in spite of the fact that Pops is living in some other realm, sleeping so much, without memory, the business empire he created continues without him. How ironic that although he is "gone," he was so powerful that his work is now being carried out through the technology of others. Dad is like a government, a political system, a corporation created by his money. With dozens of people still employed by his technology, in certain ways his money brought him the gift of immortality.

Microcosm #3: The Pelicans

At Wreck Beach, the pelicans revive a sense of the primordial. The static of busyness disappears. Having little patience with the industry of being human, I like to peer through the portal between worlds. Sometimes I have felt myself breaking through the sound barrier, passing as a heavenly being into an untampered realm. There, conception, mind and need don't exist. The unfamiliar awaits.

As I watch the pelicans, I notice that, for them, in their gliding grace, every movement is directly tied to survival. The pelicans spend their days flying, diving for fish, hunting the sea while humans are enmeshed in complex poli-economies. Why is our way so complicated, the pelicans', so simple and direct?

We will have less impoverishment when we account for ourselves and our effect on every other living creature.

love that lets us go

Oh poor man
With your rich pocket books

Oh father of quiet heart
Do you know there's nothing
Else now, but love
To fill your pockets

As we depart
Planet Earth
Into our next forms
It's love that brings us in
Love that lets us go
Into our next forms

It's faith in ceaseless life
That lets us be, always

Our answers
to survival
and prosperity
lie in the
multi-dimensional
aspects of
awareness,
in the synthesis
of science and
the ideals of spirit.

"Wingéd Life"

FREEDOM/ SAFETY

I have a cowgirl's independent spirit, requiring the random, the freedom to explore wide ranges of possibility, to ride the crest of the eternal. In the unconstricted, uncontrived moment, my mind is free to roam, examine, imagine. Freedom is essential to invention, yet requires that safe, undisturbed nest where, like in the aviary, the lovebirds' chicks are protected until fully feathered and able to fly.

Microcosm: Experiment with the Birds

Soon Wolf and I plan to commemorate a more expansive aviary that will include a small forest of eucalyptus. We are impatient to grant the parakeets, lovebirds and cockatiels more space to fly. How barbaric to limit these flying flowers to small cages. How cruel to steal the winged freedom of birds and sell them for their flightless beauty. Only the opacity of the human mind is capable of such atrocity.

One day after watching the wild birds delighting in their freedom, we decided to free our birds. We knew we could lose some of them, but the new aviary was already overpopulated; they were fighting. We felt the birds should regain their birthright, although they were in a nonindigenous environment. When something is wrong to begin with, can it ever be made right? We hoped the hawks, owls and falcons would stay away at least for awhile. I said to Wolf, as we released them, "Wouldn't you rather have one soaring flight over the seas than a lifetime of imprisonment?"

> "Wouldn't you rather have one soaring flight over the seas than a lifetime of imprisonment?"

~

Who will be the first bird out? The door is open; the boundary has been dissolved. Yet, limits still remain in the blinded eye of the programmed mind; none of the birds sees the opening. Are we not the same in our conditioning, our mental cages?

Vladimir, a parakeet, is the first to fly out. In his new glorious life regained, he shoots by us, a green fluorescent bullet soaring over the sea. Then he returns, beckoning the others; they chirp back but do not fly out, although I show them the opening. Vladimir flies back to his nest.

Have the bars and boundaries of cages programmed the birds with the imprint of a blocked life? Will the door that is now open stay closed in their minds? How long will it take humankind to open the doors of perception? Can we learn as quickly as these birds who now see the opening in their aviary and are flying freely between environments? As long as these birds can survive their predators, they will have their freedom and sanctuary — the best of both worlds. However, Nefratutu, a yellow and orange lovebird, prefers to stay home. She has the only condo left in the aviary. By remaining territorial, she is missing the possibility of freedom. She does not bother to fly about or communicate; her home is more important to her than adventure.

It is thrilling to see our parrots soar to the highest pine and eucalyptus. They fly now with the wild birds, then rejoin their relatives in the aviary.

We bless the lovebirds and hope they survive the experiment. We can not make up for the mistakes of those who cage birds, but we can give some birds back their birthright. To give the birds their freedom is to give ourselves our own, the right to our intrinsic natures.

birds in cages

Oh, birds in paradise
  feathered flowers
Your song uplifts
  the saddened heart

Man has stolen your flight
  caged your song
  within clipped wing

Bravely you still can sing
  yet as ornaments
  observed behind bars

Outside, the wild bird
  flies the breeze

You listen as a prisoner
  to their music
  from the trees

I yearn to rip off the lock
  from the door
  of your white wicker cage

But I, like you,
  am imprisoned by
  their ownership of you

Oh, the cruelties that commercialism
  so cheaply affords

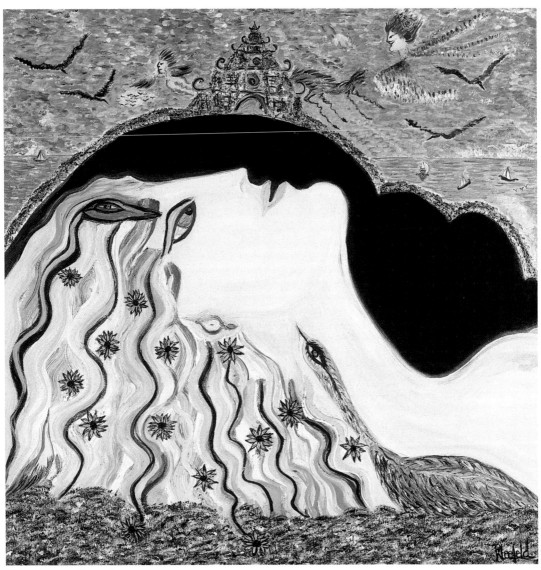

"Goddess at Home"

CHAPTER 43

KNOWING AND ACCEPTING OURSELVES

As Herman Hesse said, "All I had to do was follow my inner promptings. Why was it so difficult?"

In the intimate inner dialogue, we begin to know ourselves, to evolve a rapport with our unfamiliar thoughts and dreams. Spiritual life thrives in the innocence of the unconditioned. In the recognition of our essential nature, clarity leads us. From this awareness we may develop our personal mythology, which is ever being integrated, expanded, reaching as the tree's limbs toward the light. As we let go of desires and cravings, we become light itself, radiant, transparent creatures. Our ever-expanding comprehension becomes the invisible fiber connecting us to the Sixth Dimension.

To cultivate self-acceptance requires enduring patience and gentleness. It is in our relationship to ourselves that we can know others. To progress with those we love, we first need to embrace our own natures. Only then can we begin to understand the universe.

As I increasingly accept myself, new bonds spontaneously appear and flourish. A stronger union is created even in my existing relationships, because I know and appreciate

THE
I CHING:
58. TUI /
THE JOYOUS
A quiet, wordless, self-contained joy, desiring nothing from without and resting content with everything, remains free of all egotistic likes and dislikes. In this freedom lies good fortune, because it harbors the quiet security of a heart fortified within itself.

TAROT:
[FROM IX
THE HERMIT]
On the level of consciousness...we withdraw in order to come closer to ourselves, free and uninfluenced by the opinions of others.... The results of such experiences are an enormous growth in wisdom about life, courage, strength, and clarity.

And so, love begets love; we bring to ourselves what we are.

myself more deeply. One way to know ourselves better is to observe what and whom we gather around us.

To accept ourselves fully is also to recognize our dark side. Perhaps so-called evil is only our own shadow projected. Evil has also been described as being the Tempter. We are all capable of being dark forces as well as forces of light; it is a question of degree. How disintegrating are we in relation to others? Do we infuse others with life or alienate them?

We can only be responsible for ourselves if we are aware and courageous enough to confront our depths and heights, to really know ourselves. In the dialogue between our intimate self and our observer-self, we can embody our souls with further insights. The more in tune we are with our true nature, the more wholistic our integration, the higher our resonance. When we follow our Tao, we create less work for ourselves and others.

Microcosm: Nurturance

Recently, during a transformative experience, I received a message that I am my own mother. When I nurture myself, I can care for others.

I feel like a warrior who has come back to rest in my temple of creation. Only I can stoke the essential flames of my existence. It is time to return to basics: simple caring for myself, my loved ones, my environment.

And so, love begets love; we bring to ourselves what we are.

unnamed source

My back shapes an earthen bed
I yearn upward
My eyes ride along silvery beams, meeting planets
I am a planet myself
round, sparkling, flowing
fusing yet mercurial
My roots go far beyond self
beyond corners, boundaries
They reach, dig, branch, seed, blossom into territories
I sense but haven't seen, yet know
My roots drink from undiscovered or forgotten wells
I am part of more than I can know
I enjoy not knowing
Discoveries are constant
I am part of all that has been
is, will be
A plant, a tree of a person
My spirit soars from its source instinctively
as a wolf howls to the full moon
I am akin to the bowels of life
Its pulse races through my streams
My spirit is juicy
Its roots stand thick
in the fertile waters of where the world was born
Ah — I feel it so

"The Steppen Creatures"

CHAPTER 44

DEFINING SELF: BEING INDEPENDENT OF OTHERS' OPINIONS

It is dehumanizing to accept the role of either a worshipper or an icon. In both cases, we give away our independence.

Labels, stereotypes and categories divide us from ourselves and others. I am disinterested in being an adjective, defined by someone else's point of view. As we are more than descriptions, even "compliments" can be depersonalizing and constricting. To be a noun, however, is to be the subject of our own sentence, liberated from the judgments of others. No longer will I let another person define me.

To pursue inner dialogue, meditation and contemplation is to shed the inessential. How easy it is to lose our sensibilities when our minds wrestle with external

THE I CHING: [FROM 25. WU WANG / INNOCENCE]
*We cannot lose what really belongs to us, even if we throw it away....
we should remain true to our own natures and not listen to others.*

TAROT: [FROM XIII DEATH]
...We have reached the end of a developmental process and now must give up...our old identity. This is often a question of attitudes, opinions, and convictions that do not really have their source in our being. Instead, they have been borrowed, and often uncritically assumed, in earlier times from parents, teachers, or other role models. It is also often a matter of self-made profiles and effectively donned masks, which are now torn off in order for the true face to come to light and develop.

> As we refine
> ourselves, we
> spin our dreams
> of infinity, our
> patterns over the
> eternal seas.

affairs. If we become a cosmic noun, a planet, an orb of light, a lesser consciousness is undigestable.

In being an artist, one is of the nature of film, developing consciousness from the impressions and images of experience, casting light and shadow upon the screen of Nature's revolving transformations. As I speak of revolving, I feel the spiral of the refinement process ripple through me like music.

As we refine ourselves, we spin our dreams of infinity, our patterns over the eternal seas. We become the ever-changing hexagrams of *The I Ching*, mirroring our existences throughout time and space. If we could see this invisible existence, what a revealing spectacle it would be.

Microcosm: Releasing Preconceptions
I am giving up any preconceptions about who I am, on a constant basis. The minute my ego and pride start carrying banners of demands, insistences that lead to futile gyrations, I realize I have lost myself to the smaller, the petty, the zero-gravity spheres. My spirit wants to live as pure light, trickling in the clear streams of my existence. This transparent essence, which is my spirit-blood-marrow, moves as the infinite seas, fulfilling its mission in the interlinking of current with all life.

prelude

I want to do, be, eat, sleep, hear
without exterior reactions to my being
I want to be an invisible being,
not defined, judged, watched

I do not want to represent anything to anybody
no longer to be inside
someone's rigid picture frame of me
I want to be — just for the sense of being
To relax again enough to taste, touch, realize life
before it is filtered through to me,
through other people's psychic strainers
through their telescopic needs

I want it fresh for me to grasp
before it's had so many hands on it
Just mine to embrace, discover, share
or not share
A privacy, intimacy of me to me
whatever this may be
to relate directly from where it lies

I breathe a deep breath
at the thought of new discovery,
An intimate first-hand glide with life in my hand
with me connected directly
No filters, no microphones,
no need for closed doors; instead
Open windows, wide skies,
no hands on life's clock
Another chance to feel that part of me
that is undiluted
My life to belong to me,
to consistently feel its essence

"A Delicate Balance"

PROJECTION

IN LOVE

In relationships, especially between lovers, we become each other's mirror. We project our inner film onto the screen of those closest to us. Our unconscious emerges regardless of what our conscious mind or words say. We also project what we need to learn on those closest to us. From these unconscious projections, we can see both the dark and illumined side of ourselves.

Sometimes projection between lovers borders on madness. Who we think is our lover, is only ourselves. By realizing we produce this transference, our liberation begins. Otherwise we blame the lover, the job or the money instead of finding the origin within.

The mirrors of projection have blinded many a lover. Who could be a better reflection for our myopia than those to whom we feel closest? Even our compassion, if it exists through identification, can be merely projection. When we feel compassion, perhaps it is our self for whom we feel sorry. By becoming aware of the game of projection, we can break through this incestuous process, taking responsibility for our own lives, accepting ourselves and our peculiarities. We may then accept and better understand our loved ones and the world around us, no longer inflicting our conflicts and ignorance upon others.

Our externalized world is a reflection of our relationship to ourselves.

The mirrors of projection have blinded many a lover.

Microcosm: Wolf as Waterfall

Today Wolf is like a waterfall of spring water that I can wash my thoughts in and see them reflected. He feels pure and reflective, like a lake, noninterruptive to my cascade of rippling thought-images. I enjoy our intimate waltz of energies as we let ourselves be true to our own voices.

you were the summer

You were the summer, long before the Summer came,
Whilst the rains teemed through light and dark
Resounding the eternal water chimes
Upon my redwood roof —

You were the summer, long before the Summer came,
Entering my redwood home
Of blazing hearth
You brought another fire, smoldering
Behind your meteorites of eyes

You were the summer, long before the Summer came,
Your solar flames uncoiled
As thirsty serpent tongues, abound
Lapping my hair, my air
Consuming winter lakes
The climate changed

You were the summer, long before the Summer came,
Your long beamed fingers flew
Their currents through,
Remolding the multispheres of me

You were the summer, long before the Summer came,
Soaring to a weightless realm
We are beyond any time
            Of year

"Abstract Muse"

CHAPTER 46

RELATIONSHIP CONCEPTS

At Pfeiffer Beach in Big Sur, I watched two lovers embracing on a precipice that dropped hundreds of feet to the sea below. I thought to myself, yes, love is dangerous, when we do not know where we are; love presupposes that. To be in love is to let go of our previous concepts in order to be open, fully accepting. Feeling and intuition guide us instead of our being led by preconditioning, defenses and ideas.

Our illusions about relationship cause many of our disappointments. We have *ideas* about love, rather than trusting ourselves in the experience. We cast ourselves and others in roles that may be inappropriate. What is important is our effect on each other.

Many of today's self-help books try to make sense of love by taking the "how-to" approach. To be more than relationship technicians we need to experiment with our own beings as reference.

Why be a copy machine of unchosen material? Rather than adapting to the packaged American stereotype, why not embrace our unique expressions of love as the brushstrokes of our artistic palette, communicating in whatever style and form is natural. Being open to myriad levels of relationship allows more independence and a diversified range of interaction. We must fully

THE I CHING: 45. TS'UI / GATHERING TOGETHER

There are secret forces at work, leading together those who belong together. We must yield to this attraction; then we make no mistakes. Where inner relationships exist, no great preparations and formalities are necessary.

TAROT: XVI THE TOWER

In every case the Tower stands for a concept that used to give us a reassuring measure of security, perhaps even a feeling of safety. But now we have grown out of it. These old concepts are usually toppled.... Since this is a matter of the supposed basis of our security, these sudden changes are often first experienced as catastrophes. It is only when the first shock has been overcome that we sense with relief that we have been freed from old burdens.

May we create relationships as we would create art, continually reinventing ourselves in the process, using our imaginations rather than society's stereotypes to express our ideals.

accept our many-faceted selves. A progressive re-forming of our social attitudes and perceptions is demanded in these chaotic times.

May we create relationships as we would create art, continually reinventing ourselves in the process, using our imaginations rather than society's stereotypes to express our ideals. Love is art created. Love perpetuates reinvention.

a sublime omnipresence

O love on Earth
disguised in myriad illusion
Do you only serve
to speak of a later delusion?

Or do you sing
of a sublime omnipresence
that thrives beyond
our limited concepts
of what love is?

"Ideal Love"

CHAPTER 47

DIFFERING CAPACITIES IN LOVE

THE
I CHING:
8 PI / HOLDING
TOGETHER
What is required is that we unite with others, in order that all may complement and aid one another through holding together.

TAROT:
6 OF PENTACLES
The 6 of Pentacles stands for the qualities of helpfulness, generosity, and tolerance…. In the scope of our personal relationship the 6 of Pentacles…shows that we assist and encourage others, that we mutually help each other in difficult situations, and create a climate of generosity in that we allow the others their way of life, their success, and their joy from the depths of our heart.

Love is a most idealized and thus a most abused word. Each person has a different style yet each uses the same word to express this feeling. Other languages have numerous words for the nuances of tone and gender of love.

Our fashion of loving reflects our capacities. In other words, we may love someone yet only be capable of assisting in certain ways due to our own peculiarities. Our expressions of love depend both on our development and our inherent nature. To really love requires a generosity of being, of caring. Our relationship with ourselves, with the Cosmos, is the foundation of all other bonds.

Love thrives with trust, requiring our willingness to be vulnerable. If we are filled with past disappointments, we are not available for the new. Our parrot, Sophia, loves her mate, Nereus, although he was with Nefratutu before her. Love must be transcendental to thrive. If we live in fear of betrayal, the fear is fed and its form will manifest. It is impossible to feel trust and fear simultaneously; one vacillates between the shadows and illumined side of oneself, unable to progress in relationship.

Our relationship
with ourselves,
with the Cosmos,
is the foundation
of all other bonds.

By listening to and understanding each other, we recognize one another's abilities, diminishing the possibility of unreal expectations. In our diversity, our limits and strengths, we form a holographic circle in which we may ignite the various facets of each other's character, personality and talents.

Microcosm: Father's Day
On Father's Day I visit my ninety-two-year-old Pops. At this stage in his life, he is in another realm, unable to read his Father's Day cards or to appreciate the ritual. He could benefit far more from personal visits of loving energy, yet those who say they love him seldom visit. Although Dad cannot speak, I can be present with him by simply holding his hand, giving him the gift of care without judging his condition.

When we are ill, only a few can truly assist. Although love is easy to profess, to benefit another requires compassion, devotion and depth of understanding.

be love itself

Love is a word
with so much power
Love is a word
so much abused

Yet love's expression
is its effect

Does the one professing love
nourish your being?

Or is love's word used for control
and those who feign love,
in love with the idea of love,
unable to be love;
how can they give it?

Perhaps love is quite silent,
more genuine in behavior
    than word

"Union"

CHAPTER 48

HOLOGRAPHIC LOVE: THE IDEAL

TAROT:
ACE OF CUPS

The spectrum of the Ace of Cups extends from joy, thankfulness, and satisfaction to extreme success and the deepest happiness in oneness. The mystery of love in all its forms of expression stands, beyond all doubt, in the foreground: altruism, parental love, sensual-erotic love, self-love, and the love of God.... In the scope of our personal relationship this card of fulfillment primarily stands for the experience of true love.

The life that is spun of love's golden thread is an enriched tapestry, an ecstatic meditation. Love, like rain, moistens everything, radiating splendor. Love is our essential food, the face of the Ineffable, the One Cosmic Substance. We try to make it visible by packaging it, but its power is omnipresent. The transparency of love allows us to feel its infinite embrace, beyond a particular visibility.

Love allows us to appreciate each other regardless of our frailties or eccentricities. Yet, we may not want to respond to certain behavior. For example, narcissists, unable to give, expect others to orbit around them. In unconditional love, you can love others yet not approve of their behavior.

As the reptilians shed their skins, so do lovers in their existence together. As Nature transforms through blazes and floods, so do lovers in evolution, igniting and dissolving. Why are we so frightened of ourselves, of our shadows, when the climates themselves are reflected in our beings? In every transition, we perceive differently and thus are capable of reinventing ourselves as eternal chameleons. In reinvention, love is regenerated. To love

In reinvention,
love is
regenerated.

is to re-form ourselves as orbiting planets transfusing and reflecting one another with light and energy. Fortunately, the greater mystery remains beyond our conjecture.

Holographic love is universal in perspective. We see each other through our humaneness rather than from critical analysis and judgment. Our bonds are golden when we relate from this deeper, more expansive unity.

Holographic love means bringing all of ourselves to our love. If we are wounded or ignorant about ourselves, we bring fragments rather than wholeness to a relationship. The symptoms of the world's illnesses lurk in the broken pieces of the human body-mind-spirit.

To be caring, genuinely loving, requires an enduring nature, courageous enough to confront the ever-changing climates within. Only by transcending our survival emotions may we experience universal love, free of exploitive entrapments. I want to live in a way that lets me love as much as possible, wandering the Infinite upon Earth, my finites lost to the poetic seams of divine union.

Microcosm: The Waltz
The relationship between Wolf and me soars into an even higher love on the warm breeze of yesterday. Our love and true caring for each other transcends the ego-emotions of our human biology. This new love wave, which I reflect in my latest gold-ink-on-black-paper drawings, is a waltz of male and female energies. It asks that we move in a dance of caring regard for each other's breadth of spirit, understanding and accepting each other's unique character, letting our love go with destiny's force.

within each other's
wilderness of selves

We lived inside each other
For those fluid days and nights
Where time and sun
Were lived in
By the others

Our wicks ignited
By our sinuous flames
We were magnetically drawn, transfixed
Beyond our eyes
To each other

Our burgundy shadows
Urged silence to pulse
Our murmuring loins to fuse
Beyond selves

Curtains stayed closed
The vast blazon sky was inside
Our sensibilities breathed deeply, of
The clime in each other

The wilderness of ourselves
Wove a kingdom mounted high
In languor we were silked
Our opiate was enrapture

There were no walls, doors
Or recognizable rooms
Only in our woven kingdom
May we be contained, untamed
Within each other's wilderness of selves

"Transparent Faces"

CHAPTER 49

PARALLEL UNIVERSES IN RELATIONSHIP

TAROT:
THE FOOL
[The Fool] represents the vivacious, joyous, and uncomplicated communal way of life in which we approach each other without doubts and are always ready to discover and appreciate the many aspects of our fellow human beings.

The idea of many layers or designs of existence overlapping, interfacing with each other like separate infinite entities is fascinating to me. One may call these interrelationships parallel universes. We inhabit parallel universes as we revolve around others in unique and separate orbits. Each entity emits a unique frequency which, depending upon its alignment with another, creates harmony or cacophony. As the eminent philosopher Aldous Huxley said, "We are multiamphibians living in about twenty different worlds."

In recognizing that each orbit has a unique importance, we cease to allow competition between them. Sometimes we can integrate with each other, sometimes not.

The diversity of our species offers an endless adventure of investigation into the meaning of existence. I find it stimulating to mix with the ingredients of diverse beings. Through these interactions I recognize the myriad forces of Nature expressed in our species and reflected within.

Microcosm: Different Dialogues
Wolf and I orbit together in our reverence for Nature, the calm simplicity of our intentions providing a mutual

As the intergalactic music of eternity, we are many voices within one sound.

haven for work's play. Our independent natures free each of us to create without interruption. Our den on the Dragon's Crown* is a Noah's Ark, a sanctuary attracting a wide variety of birds and other wildlife. Our world is orchestrated amidst their songs and sounds.

I also orbit in another universe which is more scientific and analytical. In one I feel more yin; in the other, more androgynous. Parallel universes offer playgrounds of dialogue and diverse interaction where we can exercise different aspects of ourselves.

I write these thoughts as we drive up Nacimiento Road, above the Pacific. The slumbering emerald mountains surround us on this early spring afternoon.

What about the possibility of our parallel universes colliding? As this thought occurs, a car narrowly misses ours around one of the curves. Why do we assume we are separate when our worlds, consciousness, perceptions are interconnected? Here, the magic of synchronicity is again revealed. Our worlds are in orbit with the infinite constellations. I wonder what effects we are receiving from the last two visiting comets.

Our interplanetary songs resound in electronic interplay throughout time and space. As the intergalactic music of eternity, we are many voices within one sound.

in the galaxy of us

Are you assured
When we are distanced — that
We'll be together again?

When the seas of you are restless
Demanding storm,
Yearning a new moon of me
To soothe your tides
Begin again...

Are you assured
From a distance — that
We'll be together again?

And when your sun
Lights alien earth
Bruising your eyes;
Your rays bouncing back, unmet —

Are you assured
From a distance — that
We'll be together again?

Do you know
We live in each other's orbit
My earth and moon
Revolve your sun
Your beams root,
Green my gravity
And through your light
I see my moon

Knowing this you must be assured
That even when we are distanced
We are together
In the galaxy of us
    Revolving on

"Je T'Adore"

CHAPTER 50

SEXUAL

INTIMACY

One night I had a powerful dream about the coupling of male and female and was given the understanding that the relationship we have with the Sublime is our basic foundation for all others. When we are in touch with our effervescence of mission, the winds of time emit the chords of synchronicity, mysteriously drawing partners and friends to us as our essential components of mutual mission. We always meet the one from whom we can learn, as if attracting our shadow.

Sexuality is one seed of love's harvest, one facet of the holograph in which to expand and rejoice. The seed that draws lovers together in their sexuality may be their capacity to invent together, to be creative. Lovers thirst for the embrace of friendship as their bond and sexuality as their creative seed. We, as lovers, blend our beings, and in definition of each other, know more about ourselves.

Devoted love endures many transitions of sexuality and friendship. Sometimes, if we evolve differently, our passion for sexual intimacy cools. If we view these transitions as changes of form, rather than as endings, our bond can evolve to another level with less suffering.

Possessive love smothers. Ego, false pride and expectation are futile; the universal process asks that we, as lovers in evolution, transcend these stagnant emotional patterns.

TAROT: 9 OF CUPS
The 9 of Cups stands for a time that we deeply savor and enjoy from the heart. Although this love of life can occasionally get out of hand in exaggerations such as lust or greed...in the moderate form this card shows...a time of carefree existence. It is a time in which we turn our eyes to the beautiful things of this world...In the scope of personal relationship this card indicates a happy time of delightful enjoyment. The fantasies, usually only associated with vacation experiences or the dream of a lonely island, now become what we experience in every day life.

Our sexuality is grounded in our survival instincts, but when we express those feelings with the light of true love, they become nurturing, powerful and transcendent.

If we bring fear and distrust, we lose what we have. Love is as fragile as creation; it is spun of the great mystery, the invisible ingredients. As architects of our personal mythology, we shed our egoistic, sexist habits, regenerating our deepest heart to weave a poetic story.

Within the black stallions of the wild winds, sexual instinct is lusty, fully savage. Within the human, sexual instinct can be just as uninhibited, but the static, possessive games that may follow destroy the chemistry of magical connection. Our sexuality is grounded in our survival instincts, but when we express those feelings with the light of true love, they become nurturing, powerful and transcendent. Without corruptive emotions, intimate sexuality can thrive.

Microcosm: A Blend of Selves
I feel my most expansive in my intimacy with Wolf. The more we trust our love, ourselves, the more exquisite is our loving. In nurturing love as our elixir of ecstasy, we spawn its seeds.

We anoint each other in our ripening nectars. Wolf becomes the river god Nereus who guards the Earth's rivers. I become a daughter of Neptune, a sea goddess; in receptivity we liquify our love. Bathing in the moon's iridescence, we play like the wild creatures we live among, hungrily nibbling each other. Winter becomes summer in the suns that blossom within us.

Eggs, figs, mangoes are in abundance. Meadows of wildflowers incense our blood-sap; our den is a fragrant womb. We have woven our gossamer threads into our cocoon-den.

We return to our deepest natures, to simplicity. I realize how disturbed we have become by the corruptive demands of other realities, our intimacy torn, invaded by the complexities of human striving. These inexplicable forces have taken two wild creatures away from their love-mating rhythms, away from the balm of ecstasy, their pollination.

To love Wolf is to return to the eucalyptus forests with the red roses blooming. Again we vow to nurture our flower-selves daily. We have said this often and then been blown off course by the winds of human-busyness. Yet in every note of our living, love is in our glance, our touch, our song, in the deep tidepools of the intimate. Our intimacy is an offering to our altars within. Our creativity is love returned, bountiful after the violent winds, the droughts of withdrawal.

Fragranced with the pollen of intimacy, we cover ourselves in roses from a bedroom vase. Why does psychology cast a biased view on symbiosis? A blending of selves is an essential ingredient in the soaring of two souls.

Love is as fragile as creation; it is spun of the great mystery, the invisible ingredients.

to make of the love that unshadows the moon

You lie on a white beach
In your white slacks
And the command,
The insistence of
Your intensity,
Your muscular silence
Speaks of an urgency
Of a desire
To make love...

To make of the love
That unshadows the moon
The red love
That inflames the mind
Soaring it
Beyond this sun

The making of a love
That swirls
Our two planets
To a further constellation
Of our selves

This insistence of
Your intensity
This muscular silence
That speaks in urgency
Behind your white clothes
Commands the desire
For this kind of love

In nurturing love as
our elixir of ecstasy,
we spawn its seeds.

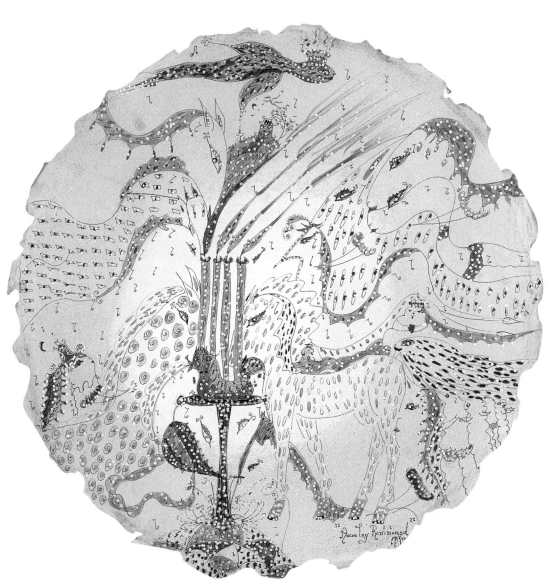

"Ancestry Revisioned"

CHAPTER 51

ANCESTRY

REVISIONED

THE
I CHING:
37. CHIA JÊN /
THE FAMILY
[THE CLAN]
*When the family is in
order, all the social
relationships of mankind
will be in order.*

As I reunite with my past, I see into the early seeds of
childhood, my genetics, my cycles of evolving. In so doing,
I learn about myself from my beginnings, about the
behaviors, influences of my family and friends. As I study
the origins and the strange mix of my ancestors' alchemy,
I better understand my own ingredients. From a distance,
I view how one cycle led me into the next, an accumulation
of experience fueling progression.

I see that in my childhood I was engaged in the same primary
activities as now. How my mind and imagination worked is
recorded in my early letters, drawings and stories, revealing
the nucleus, the psychology of who I am now. I see that I
always had a passion for wilderness and wildlife, that I was
a born wanderer intuitively drawn to discovery through
observing the natural world, people and myself. A great
curiosity always propelled my mind.

As I travel into the past I see how I have shed, through
time, the preconditioning, the faulty prescriptions, growing younger as I grow older; the passions of my early life
are the immortal seeds of my todays.

As I gather the gems of wisdom that gild my soul, I am
both encouraged and astonished by how tenacious life is.
Somehow through the greatest challenges our essential nature
endures and refines. I see how gradual is the carving of one's
philosopher's stone. I trust more than ever the flow of life.

I stand as a willow tree, bending low to the Earth, to the nourishment and wisdom my ancestors have borne.

As I examine the records, the skins of past history shed, I see the I Change as the Invisible Chameleon.

Microcosm: My Inner Architecture Revealed

I inherited two opposite tendencies: my mother's artistic temperament and my father's pioneering business acumen. Adding to this alchemy, my father's grandfather was a rabbi in Poland, and my mother's father was a musician in Portugal. I also inherited a lineage of oppressed females on my mother's side, some of whom committed suicide. My mother's German mother was not allowed downstairs until her less attractive sisters were married. My mother's feeling of resignation in giving up her art career to have children had a profound effect on my resolve to live differently. I feel my drive for artistic expression is partially propelled by my mother, that I am in a sense liberating my female ancestors today from what they suffered yesterday.

Usually, my art precedes my consciousness, letting me know that I am entering a new phase. At a recent meeting with attorneys involving family issues, I detached my energy and drew some innovative architectural houses and a boat. These sketches spoke to me of the new structure I was creating in my living, the defining of my inner architecture. The Sixth Dimension is my realm of ideals; I draw myself into its future.

I notice the humor in the drawing for this chapter entitled *Ancestry Revisioned*. In it, I depict myself, my essence as a peculiar, small creature on a platter with candles rising from me. Symbolically I offered myself on a platter, hoping to bring harmony to my family. This odd little creature on the platter has the same pointed ears and needle-like beak as the Witness of the More. I was encouraged to see this detached aspect of myself in action.

This past twelve-year cycle, originally catalyzed by an alienation between my father and me, has now culminated in a blessed reunion. I am re-examining the past, my karma, my family and its underlying dynamics — money issues, value systems, the old world. I bring with me the harvest of many years of cultivation.

I stand as a willow tree, bending low to the Earth, to the nourishment and wisdom my ancestors have borne. Slowly their alchemy is stirred in the cauldron within, always a slightly different mixture emerges, evolving as me.

The neuroconspiratorial games of some of my family are those of the world's hierarchies, bred by fear and the need to control. Yet, through illumination the past is revealed, its illusions, projections and outworn influences. We are liberated to begin again. May we collaborate with those of kindred values, those whose incentives are of the spirit.

As I travel into the past I see how I have shed, through time, the preconditioning, the faulty prescriptions, growing younger as I grow older; the passions of my early life are the immortal seeds of my todays.

the desert of myself

Wind-spun into existence
A cold and alien child, storm-fed
Stumbles through the desert of herself
Vacant in the starless void

Hurled face-flat upon the desert
Roots dry and withering
The granules of sand speak in primal tone;
They teach a sacred and ancient text
Which otherwise could not be known:

> The past is but a mirage
> A wellspring of illusion;
> Your memories will be grasped
> By fiery thrusts of hailing stone

The cold and alien child stumbles on
Overturning the sands of her interior
Slowly decoding the equations
Of her essential nature

Until what seemed an eternity passes
And the weary child dawn-awakens
To a resplendent sun
Her vacancy breathed away
Her being courage-bronzed

Eyelashed in the dew of origin
The child and the parent are one again
And this new one re-enters the Garden of Eden

I depict myself, my essence, as a peculiar, small creature on a platter with candles rising from me. Symbolically, I offered myself on a platter, hoping to bring harmony to my family.

"Angels of Innocence"

CHAPTER 52

LEADERS

Why do we feel the need to fit into consensus reality? We are a world of people all seeking each other's approval, yet few answer to themselves. Is it our lack of self-acceptance that causes us to seek others' authority and definition before we look into our own eyes?

Why do so many people assume a dependent position? Perhaps the old child within remembers looking up to others who seemed to have all the answers. Why do we need to idolize? The answers appear to be both psychological and biological. Our species, instinctively herd-like, is also exposed to extreme psychological manipulations. Society's hierarchies, including familial, religious and governmental, demand, expect us to conform, and the one who takes a different path is labeled an outsider, an oddball.

Benjamin DeCasseres says in his book *Chameleon* that history is the forces of Nature dressed up. Because the forces of Nature are played out through us, we are vehicles, vessels of the vaster essence. In the alchemical theater, we play out our roles in dress and personality.

The leaders we choose to represent our values and biases are external representatives of our bodies' internal politics. Sometimes the forces that inhabit us are raw, naked and primitive. Often we create celebrities to serve as surrogates for the expression of our own frustration, ambition and suppressed aggression. We also project our shadow side onto idols who, as puppets, act out our unconscious strivings.

THE
I CHING:
34. TA CHUANG /
THE POWER OF
THE GREAT
The hexagram points to a time when inner worth mounts with great force and comes to power...that is truly great power which does not degenerate into mere force but remains inwardly united with the fundamental principles of right and of justice.

TAROT:
KING OF WANDS
This card is an expression of power of the will, self-assurance, idealistic striving for growth, and the great possible development and maturation of person... combining a claim to leadership with the appropriate qualifications.

True authority is authorship for oneself.

Even our more inspired and aware leaders often live in the concrete density provided by the others. It appears the most aggressive and control-driven people shape politics, make history and profit from it. We are born into a world in which most authorities attempt to dull and confuse us. Generally, their expensive prescriptions are poisons of ignorance: hypocrisy and exploitation, resulting in indiscriminate control and emotional abuse.

Some of our so-called healers are shams rather than shamans, strategy-oriented technicians misleading their followers for self-promotion. Their belief systems, which they project as unconditional love, are tools used to exploit others. They often disguise themselves in "spirituality" doing business even with God. They are "smugglers of the soul," as DeCasseres put it, preying on the fear, guilt and despair of others.

As always, it is up to the individual. Genuine process is not the imitation of another's beliefs. When we cease adapting to the modes of others and projecting our subconscious needs and desires onto "leaders," we can make significant changes in ourselves and the world.

To be leaders in the true sense, we need to construct a personal philosophy, weaving the threads of our personal integration into the Cosmic Loom. In our courage to experiment, to treat life as an adventure, leadership may evolve. True authority is authorship for oneself. By cultivating our compassion and wisdom, we become leaders by example, manifesting our highest potential both singularly and collectively.

letter to rimbaud

Yes, Rimbaud,
the inanities of being a human
stick like flies

Will there ever be a time
of being comfortable with
what humanity is —
with living as a human?

It appears there is an endless stumbling
starting with one's first steps in childhood
Tripping, falling, stepping, climbing —
There at last is adulthood,
the grown child comes face to face
with an approaching end
and sees the movie of illusions fade and leave

Old memories that now are eased,
left to the webs of time
Relieved to be deserted on the shores
of an unknown tomorrow
A body that no longer grasps
for outworn ideals

Inner myth is left to the stars
No trace of the defeat except
in the stories of the interpreters
who can not know what this
unusual spirit experienced

Yes, you Rimbaud
are supreme
in your refined translation
        of the raw

"Dream of the Auburn Hair"

CHAPTER 53

UTOPIAN VISIONS

We have reached a time and place in our history where progress is possible only if the human species is willing to change. For life to go on, the planet must move to a higher state of integration and refinement. We need to scrutinize our thinking and eliminate the alibis of blame and excuse. In our humanness lies the capacity for all that exists. May we stoke those fires into brilliance that illuminate revelations of enlightened meaning. As *The I Ching* states, "Greatness and justice must be united indissolubly."

We must each account for our every interaction and its effect. By sustaining an ideal ecology, an ideal politics within, so our world will change. As an extension of our consciousness, our technology will offer more organic systems* that will assist individuals and the cooperative whole. Instead of exploiting each other or our planet, let us be in symbiotic co-creation with the Earth's pulse, evolving into the Sixth Dimension. In living this wisdom, we emancipate ourselves from our human bondage, sculpting our character, our Earth.

In our divided world, the universal soul is injured. We erupt as volcanoes to repair worlds. Division can not survive. May we dissolve the arbitrary boundaries of our countries, of our souls. In building bridges of compassion, we transcend the separation of defense.

THE I CHING:
11. TAI / PEACE

This hexagram denotes a time in nature when heaven seems to be on earth.... When the spirit of heaven rules in man, his animal nature also comes under its influence and takes its appropriate place.... Heaven and earth are in contact and combine their influences, producing a time of universal flowering and prosperity.

TAROT:
XVII THE STAR

The Star is the card of hope, wisdom, and insight into higher correlations.... This is a matter of deep insights in a greater context, through which we grow beyond the narrowness of our immediate horizon... (It) signifies promising encounters and propitious connections that are stimulating and hold a future for us.

* see glossary

The unified pulse of every human creature will bring us to our next stage of evolution.

In communicating honestly with the intention to unify, we will be receptive to each other's expression, to the language of All.

Every living thing has tendrils reaching out in all directions. Each pebble that drops adds another current to infinity's pools. So it is that each person's suffering can be felt by all. The unified pulse of every human creature will bring us to our next stage of evolution. When people have the intention to unify, refusing division and the resulting wars, issues can be creatively resolved.

Love, the indivisible Cupid, connects us in our diversity, inspiring union as our primary intention, liberating us. As radiant people in cadence, we are sound waves attracting each other's harmonious currents. May each of our tones resonate from our clearest light, recording the New History, the land of imagination, the holographic synthesis of perspectives, the soul in its garlands manifested in science.

weightless light

You and I
as Indians we live

When in our finest tune
we weave electric notes of poetry,
metabolize their scores,
compose sunset palaces,
metallic future cities
where radiance orbs
beyond myopia
where wilderness-vision thrives
in pulsing resonance of singing light

Clear attitudes of altitude:
Spheres of perception in orbit

"Galactic Femme"

CHAPTER 54

RELATING

TO EARTH

AS A BEING

TAROT:
XXI THE WORLD
*The World shows the unity
that has been regained,
the experience of greatest
harmony, and the
joyful conclusion of a
development.... In terms
of external experiences
this means that we have
found our place, the place
where we simply belong.
On the level of inner
experiences, this card
shows that we have taken
a significant, perhaps even
decisive step toward
becoming who we are,
toward true authenticity
and wholeness.*

The Earth asks me to be here as her honored guest. My streams resonate from the Earth's shores as I embrace Gaia as myself, as a constellation webbed within eternity.

I think of the Earth-Body as a transforming Being with an intergalactic, integrating intelligence, ever in meditation and chaos, living in the natural coincidence of fusion.

Climates may be considered as the Earth-Body's feelings emoting transformation for survival. The Earth's health is one with ours. Our sensitivity to Gaia is analogous to our sensitivity to ourselves and others. When we war with the Tao, we distort ourselves and defile our planet.

We have polluted much of the land, oceans and air. In contaminating our Earth-Body, we bite the hand that feeds us, destroying innumerable species. We produce massive amounts of waste, much of it nonbiodegradable, symptomatic of blatant disregard.

The dolphin, whale and elephant, with their larger brains, earlier origins and longer histories, cohabit more peacefully. Because we are only one percent genetically different from the chimpanzee, it is no wonder we often

> I think of the
> Earth-Body as
> a transforming
> Being with an
> intergalactic,
> integrating
> intelligence.

behave like primitives in a world zoo. I recognize in myself the primitive rawness of the archetypal forces. I attempt not to spread any of my own viruses of being, but sometimes they can be overwhelming. Are the forces of Nature simply being expressed through us? Are we the involuntary instruments of evolution, or is it de-evolution?

Humans have always been a chaos-generating species, even twenty-five hundred years ago when the founder of Taoism, Lao Tzu, recorded his profound teachings. Perhaps this is our function, to steer between the complexities of chaos and order, to be the fountainheads of creation. Perhaps we are not as polluted and distorted as it appears, but merely the well-worn tools of Nature's infinite garden. Nature can be senseless, ruthless and torturous, so why should we be any different. On this planet, the barbaric appears to be part of evolution, along with the visionary. Each dynamic contributes life and death forces to the infinite organism. The Grand Intelligence uses us as Its tools, whenever and however It needs. How ludicrous to imagine that we are in charge of more than the finites when the Earth and the galactic systems are the Sublime in Undesign or the Cosmic Coincidence Control, as Dr. John Lilly terms it.

Earth transitions through physical phenomena, climatic change and catastrophes, drawing what is needed to regain balance, to evolve. Transition requires some form of destruction. Nature forces the rusted elements of our corrupt systems to falter and break, requiring us to create "a new way of thinking," as Albert Einstein once said. We transform ourselves as does our Earth, as one whole organism.

Just as in any illness, the Earth-Body and its inhabitants will heal from their healthy parts. Already the Lover-Healer is moving to the next stage of evolution, where the environment will be nutrified with essential life ingredients, our spirit-manifestations mirroring our ever-spiraling clarity. There will be a refining of forms, but not death as we know it. In this Sixth Dimension neither needs nor hunger exists. We will manufacture our own chlorophyll and be able to digest nutrients through our breathing. We will no longer be the predators of a planet, but will contribute to the atmosphere, the cosmic flora and fauna, living in symbiotic union with all of creation. Our energies will be the nutrients for each other, without destruction. Those in resonance with the Life Force are already released from the pollution of anger, greed and envy — the gravity of viral emotions.

As wards of the Cosmos, we are in the bottleneck of evolution. May we dedicate ourselves to a *new way of thinking,* to a new humanism. The survival of today's world is dependent on our awareness. Dr. Carl Jung stated that, "The universe hangs by a thread, and that thread is man's psyche." As the eternal wildflowers of Creation's experiment, we are seeds of the vast unfolding.

Microcosm: Climates of the Mind

The climates of Earth are in dialogue with the climates of our bodies. We are inseparable from Nature. I realize more now what the title of my first book, *Climates of the Mind,* really means. It is saying that the planet's climates are exhibited through us; we are her avatars.

Psychological, biological and emotional explanations exist for the cause of an effect. But now that I identify my feelings with the Earth's, I better understand the power, the impact that I, at times, feel forced to endure.

Perhaps this is our function, to steer between the complexities of chaos and order, to be the fountainheads of creation.

Earth transitions
through physical
phenomena,
climatic change
and catastrophes,
drawing what is
needed to regain
balance, to evolve.

When I am having a subjective, personal experience,
I am also tuning into the universal. This is true for all
of us as sensitive receptors. Nothing is only personal
as some people imply, as if that makes it of less value.
We can not have the microcosm without the macrocosm.

the splendorous feel of the infinities

Fields of wild stars
Wreathe the drowsy mountains
Their astral bloom ascends
In the global gardens of space

Galaxies spiral of glittering blossoms
Their pollen casts an illumined path
Across the fathomless dome

Silvery petals cascade
Liquid tides of black horizon
Amidst beacons of transient ships at sea

The ebony mountains of night slumber
As colossal beasts who once dwelled in ancient seas
Now they bask in thick waves of earthly heat
Dazzling blossoms constellate their forested crowns

The nectar of their inner streams
Trickles in the ripened summer
Moistening their sculptured flanks
Waterfalling to the seas below

One is touched
By the maverick currents
Of soundless laughter,
The splendorous feel of the infinities

"The Door"

CHAPTER 55

PIERCING THE MEMBRANE

Our connection with the Sublime is our foundation for all other relationships. Concepts, beliefs and illusions are but ripples reflecting this primary relationship.

When we transcend our mental and physical limitations, we move to the Divine Ground, becoming the *Atman** within the infinite order of Creation. Within this sublime experience, the molecular technologies of existence may be revealed. In the radiance of these illuminations, we comprehend the underlying forces. In the resonant sensibility of interlinking chords, a certain intelligence arises, the gentleness of integrated comprehension.

May we behold the miracle of our vast natures, in alignment with the Intergalactic Technology. Krishnamurti says, "It is not important to discuss what lies beyond, because we are discussing a thing which is unconditioned with a conditioned mind." But, it is important to experience what lies beyond.

We breathe our kingdom into being when we go beyond the seams into the Sixth Dimension where all is possible. From there life is beheld in its molecular transparency as continuous bubbles of possibility. This seeing through and into makes me think of us as mind explorers diving into the atoms of the ocean floor, then peering up into myriad sunlit realities. We trespass the mere appearance

---

THE I CHING: 20. KUAN / CONTEMPLATION (VIEW)

Contemplation of the divine meaning underlying the workings of the universe gives to the man who is called upon to influence others the means of producing like effects.... It enables them to apprehend the mysterious and divine laws of life, and by means of profoundest inner concentration they give expression to these laws in their own persons. Thus a hidden spiritual power emanates from them....

TAROT: KING OF CUPS

The King of Cups embodies...our search for transcendental experience, redemption, and the mysterious unification with the original source....

---

* see glossary

> We trespass the mere appearance of something, seeing into its root with vision, the illumination of deeper comprehension.

～

of something, seeing into its root with vision, the illumination of deeper comprehension. In the world of crystalline meaning, we ride our flaming current; our kaleidoscope of perception is resilient yet focused, and miracles tumbleweed, evolving our personal mythology.

Microcosm: Imprinted With the Absolute

When Wolf mentions the worlds that may exist beyond the visible, I feel myself looking as if with laser sight into the skies, through cocoons of light, into unfolding color, into a gauzy lightness. I see the molecular structure of everything, the jet trail that my hand leaves when it moves through the air. I see color as life's chemistry, as musical chords that voice the song.

The oak moths flutter as diaphanous flowers, illuminated by the sun. Resting on a lounge chair, gazing into the twittering wings of Nature's invisible breath, I bask in the unlimited. The fathomless seas echo resonant tides, as my currents dance in the shimmer of the pines' crowns, in the incessant buzz and chirp.

Of late, I have felt imprinted by the Absolute. I can let myself be without interference. My sensibilities are drawn to subtlety, ecstasy, detachment, the simplicity that is the Divine Ground, the seamless space that gestates the human seed.

On a paradisiacal afternoon, I lie stretched upon a dry carpet of pine needles. The sentinel trees of Indian spirit filter golden beams through their boughs. I let myself pass through the membrane of limited dimension into the unbounded.

prevails a microcosmic soul

In the heavens' wilderness primordial
High beyond miasmic grasp
Where barely a human's thumbprint tracks
Prevails a microcosmic soul
Imbuing magnitude unbounded
Breathing primal symphonies of
Orphic breeze and Zephyr's wind
Feathering the wingéd seed

O genesis of life
Beyond man's demise
You are an aliment for fervent spirits
Impassioned of the blazing eye
Recreating life as the heavens live

O eternal Renaissance of reincarnations
You scintillate infinite transformations
Veining matter into rhythm's marrow of form

O microcosmic soul; domed countenance
Within your illimitable cathedral
Of sovereign being,
You answer not
For drought or storms
Nor lightning's charring cleave

O spirit translucent
Who bodes in the wake of torch's day
Your face exudes primordial temperaments
Effusing your boundless cathedral
Complexioning archetype and myth
In artless design

O conveyor of evanescent perfection
You are eternal in
Your sublime shadow of expression

"Astro-Divers"

CHAPTER 56

BECOMING

DENIZENS

OF OTHER

DIMENSIONS

As I peer into words, their origins and meanings, I better understand the multidimensionality of our codes of existence. The word ecstasy is rooted in the Greek words *ek,* meaning "out," and *histanai,* meaning "to place." When we are experiencing the rapture and delight of ecstasy, we are literally "stepping out of our immediate, physical place," into a realm of the spirit. We become multidimensional, both of the world and beyond it. Out of holographic vision comes the Sixth Dimension, liberation from the closed doors of consensus reality.

Hermann Hesse's book, *The Glass Bead Game,* could be interpreted as a look through the kaleidoscope of existence, creating the ultimate from the Overview, the code of the Sixth Dimension, the Paradise of Possibility.

We can be the overseers of multidimensional universes, each in dialogue with the others. In our capacity to perceive the Overview, to comprehend parallel universes,

THE
I CHING:
24. FU / RETURN
(THE TURNING
POINT)
After a time of decay comes the turning point. The powerful light that has been banished returns.... The old is discarded and the new is introduced.... Societies of people sharing the same views are formed. But since these groups... are in harmony with the time, all selfish separatist tendencies are excluded, and no mistake is made.

TAROT:
XIX THE SUN
[This card] represents an awakening, the blossoming and maturing of our sun-related nature, which can be compared to our true self. All of the qualities connected with this concept can be found here: self-assurance...knowledge of oneself, independence, as well as the mature ability to rise above oneself and attain a wise state of selflessness.

In our capacity
to perceive the
Overview, to
comprehend
parallel universes,
we see through
the architecture
of our realities,
becoming
denizens of the
Sixth Dimension.

we see through the architecture of our realities, becoming denizens of the Sixth Dimension, creating a mythology of ecstasy while still on planet Earth.

In the Sixth Dimension, Primal Spirit Intelligence manifests universal structures, technologies. These structures exist beyond our present sight as the gossamer architecture of the new biology, evolving as we are, awaiting our next forms.

The journey of mystical enlightenment is the alchemy of possibility, guiding us as we explore the Sixth Dimension. There, attitude determines altitude. Although we attempt navigation, it is not within our control; the energy takes us where we must go. In this realm, competition, greed, envy, the convolutions of primitive instincts no longer exist. Love is the unifying substance. The illumined reveal themselves. Philosophic ideals pulse our way of living. In the Sixth Dimension, we see the past and the future coexisting with the present.

As architects of dimensional perspectives, we see through the universe, how it functions on a basic level, connecting us to what William Blake termed the "reality beyond the senses." In understanding that the laws of physics apply to our psycho-biological beings, we see that "Atoms Mirror Atoms," that the energy we put out will return in kind. The winds, fires and floods that fuel the universe are also the voices of our souls; there is no separation except in form.

The life of the Invisible is unlimited, far beyond the sight of eye, beyond our narrow-lensed interpretations of physical reality. The Sixth Dimension is for society's evolutionary mutants, the visionaries, the explorers and the innovators. There are no fragmented systems, only ourselves on a tightrope in space, in symbiotic yet independent union with all that exists. Our balance is our interconnection with the universe, with all others.

We are cosmic dancers holding hands in space, our songs ascending in eternal symphony. Our suspension is supported by our interconnection with the Invisible Forces that be.

The winds, fires and floods that fuel the universe are also the voices of our souls; there is no separation except in form.

the timeless beams

The beams of my centered star
reach into timelessness

The abundant moment of me
fills the universe

My rays fuse
with celestial beings

Flight feathers my arms
soaring me beyond origin

Countless leaves of me
fly into breezes

Never to land
only transform

As the skies' countenance
ever changes
Nomadic sands
ever drift
So it is

My path thus sublimely lit
crystal clear in purity, purpose

I breathe expanded
in the open temple of myself

The ultimate of knowing
the eternal

Our suspension
is supported by
our interconnection
with the Invisible
Forces that be.

LIST *of* IMAGES *(selected from the years 1986-1997)*

LIST of POEMS *(selected from the years 1974-1997)*

REFERENCED BOOKS

Banzhaf, Hajo.
The Tarot Handbook.
Christine M. Grimm, trans.
Stamford: U.S. Games Systems, 1993

Bedford, Sybille.
Aldous Huxley: A Biography.
New York: Knopf, 1974.

Blake, William.
*The Complete Poetry & Prose
of William Blake, Rev. Ed.*
David V. Erdman, ed.
Berkeley: University of California Press,
1981.

Blau, Evelyne.
Krishnamurti: 100 Years.
New York: Stewart, Tabori & Chang,
1995.

Bosker, Ben Z. and Bosker, Baruch M., eds.
Talmud: Selected Writings.
Mahwah, NJ: Paulist Press, 1989.

Dawkins, Richard.
The Selfish Gene.
New York: Oxford Univ. Press, 1990.

De Casseres, Benjamin.
The Chameleon.
New York: Lieber & Lewis, 1922.

Drexler, Eric.
Engines of Creation.
New York: Anchor/Doubleday, 1987.

Hess, Thomas B., ed.
*The Grand Eccentrics: Five Centuries of
Artists Outside the Main Currents of Art.*
(Art News Annual XXXII).
New York: Macmillan, 1966.

Hesse, Herman.
Magister Ludi or The Glass Bead Game.
Richard and Clara Winston, trans.
New York: Holt, Rinehart & Winston,
1969.

Huxley, Laura.
This Timeless Moment.
New York: Farrar, Strauss & Giroux,
1968.

Jeffers, Robinson.
*Collected Poems of Robinson Jeffers,
Vols. I & II.*
Stanford: Stanford Univ. Press,
1988 & 1989.

Lilly, John, M.D.
*"Programming and Metaprogramming
in the Human Bio-Computer."*
San Francisco: The Whole Earth
Catalog, 1964.

Rilke, Rainer Maria.
Letters to a Young Poet.
Stephen Mitchell, trans.
New York: Random House, 1986.

Rilke, Rainer Maria.
Translated Poetry of Rainer Maria Rilke.
Stephen Mitchell, ed. and trans.
New York: Vintage, International, 1989.

Van Gogh, Vincent.
*Dear Theo: The Autobiography of
Vincent Van Gogh.*
Irving Stone and Jean Stone, eds.
New York: New American Library/
Dutton, 1995.

Wilhelm, Richard, trans.
The I Ching or Book of Changes.
Cary F. Baynes, trans.
Princeton: Princeton University Press,
1977.

Willens, Harold.
*The Trimtab Factor: How Business
Executives Can Help Solve the Nuclear
Weapons Crisis.*
New York: William Morrow, 1984.

GLOSSARY *of* KEY CONCEPTS & CHARACTERS

Atman   From the Sanskrit, meaning the individual soul, the principle of life or the supreme and universal soul from which all individual souls arise.

Atoms Mirror Atoms   We are constantly cloning ourselves emotionally, physically and spiritually in our actions, thoughts and cars. We are copy machines, duplicating our inner technology in the exterior. This theory expresses a poetic synthesis of some key principles of religion and physics: Every action has an equal and opposite reaction; What you sow, so shall you reap; Like not only attracts, but begets like. *(See Chapter 22: "Atoms Mirror Atoms.")*

Deltas of Apollo   *Deltas of Apollo* is an inner landscape, an astral land. The painting also speaks to me in terms of the Earth, its health and our health. It represents the end of the Earth as we know it. The nature of the Earth itself is insisting that we move into our next stage of evolution, a transition that will transcend the present limitations of our biology. The title, *Deltas of Apollo*, translates as a plea for humankind to bring all inherent possibility to a higher refinement of being, a balance of body, mind and spirit. (See painting on p. *viii*.)

The Dragon's Crown   The location of my home at the top of a dragon-shaped mountain in the coastal wilderness of Monterey County in California.

Editorial Owl   The wise owl of us that can discriminate and edit the superfluous ingredients of life. *(See Chapter 7: "Editing, Sifting, Refining.")*

The I Change   The I Change, inherent in every one of us, is the invisible chameleon within, a vapor-like essence made up of all that has ever been and will be. When our perceptions change, we see things differently. And when we see things differently, we evolve. The process is an endless one of surfing and navigating the realities of existence. Ultimately, we are all eye in the shifting light of consciousness.

Meme   This term was coined by British biologist Richard Dawkins in 1976 to mean a unit of information that is carried from one person to another. This is a cultural phenomenon transmitted by repetition similar to the way genes replicate biologically.

Macro-Micro Theory   We are truly microcosms of the Macrocosm. As in our immune system, complex and diversified political systems literally run our lives, just as we see in our environment. Every interior function that is needed to keep us alive is also duplicated in our outer world. We have cops, robbers, nurses, judges, tyrants and slaves seething in our cauldrons, replicated within and without.

This theory can help to explain the peculiarities of the human species. *(See Chapter 22: "Atoms Mirror Atoms.")*

Microcosm   Particularly refers to the personal experience of the author.

Nabis   From the Hebrew, meaning "prophet": an avante-garde group of artists who lived in the late 1800s and early 1900s and were considered to be the forerunners of modernism.

Organic Systems   For more information on computer and communication systems which synthesize the organic and the technological, contact Francis Jeffrey at Elfnet, Inc., PO Box 6844, Malibu, California 90264.

Pankosmion   From the Greek, meaning "place of the whole universe," the name of my mountaintop home, a Garden of Eden where the chrysalis is ever becoming the butterfly, where the guardians protect the soul's treasures.

The Sixth Dimension   The realm where death as we know it does not exist, where violence has no pulse, where there is no time and one lives in the eternal, where body, mind and spirit are in a continual process of regeneration. The Garden of Eden restored to its sapience of origin; the quantum math of the complete; the rhapsody of ecstasy; the timeless gift bestown of our birth.

(See Chapter 22: "Atoms Mirror Atoms", Chapter 55: "Piercing the Membrane" and Chapter 56: "Becoming Denizens of Other Dimensions.")

Trimtab   From Harold Willens' book, *The Trimtab Factor,* a nautical / aeronautical term referring to the ability to leverage something large or important, or both, with a small but crucial force. In the same way, small but crucial private acts can change the course of history.

Unique Enzymes   Each one of us is a unique enzyme, a specific and predestined agent expressing Nature's chemistry. As such, each of us is a vital ingredient in the alchemy of life. This concept helps to explain the diversity of the human species. Our preordained genetic code, along with our consciousness, directs the films of our essential natures. If we can peer into our genetic code and comprehend our messenger-type, we will know ourselves better, become wiser and better understand the inner, thus outer dynamics of the world around us. *(See Chapter 23: "Genetic Codes.")*

Voidoid   One who appreciates the value of the empty mind and of being an instrument of the Divine.

The Witness of the More   The Witness of the More, whose perceptions come from the Overview, is the observer of our Theater of Illusion, our guardian who remains objective, detached. Ideally, each of us has this personal yet impersonal guardian on duty as needed. In my drawings I depict this aspect of the I Change as a creature with pointed ears and a triangular face with a distinctive needle beak. The Inflammable Witness of the More is another character description of the Witness of the More, emphasizing the ability to remain a cool enough observer not to get burned. *(See also the image, "The Witness of the More Sees with Golden Seeds," in Chapter 5: "The Overmind View.")*

Wolf A godparent of this book, a kin of my soul, also referred to as Nereus.

Zen Voidoid An eternal wanderer and explorer who lives spontaneously, orchestrated by sublime intuition; one who knows the void as receptive mind. The Zen Voidoid prefers living in a state of exalted mystery, letting the Tao lead the way.

OTHER BOOKS *and* WORK *by the* AUTHOR
Available from Merrill-West Publishing

Climates of the Mind
"Here is a rare wedding of poetry, philosophy, and psychological awareness, without the wooden self-consciousness of most modern psychological writing.... A human document. It touches the deepest places.... Informs and potentially heals its readers by communicating with love, a sense of what underlies the particulars of their lives...this book will live."
— From the Foreword, Carl A. Faber, Ph.D., Psychologist and Author

Satan Sleeps with the Holy: Word Paintings
"Ms. Kleefeld provides an invaluable gift, a proclamation of the power of the human soul... This numinous poet probes such universal concerns as the nature of Truth, Passivity, Ignorance, Tyranny, Love, Integrity, Courage.... She metabolizes Nature, its quintessential Truth...and emerges as do those rare few, as a keeper and communicator of the God-fires. Other brave and noble souls may so be inspired."
— From the Introduction, Patricia Holt, Publisher

Lovers in Evolution
"In Carolyn Kleefeld's opus, *Lovers in Evolution,* the spiritual and the sensual merge without contradiction in a vast love encompassing nature, the universe, change, oneself, and the beloved."
— Francis Jeffrey, Author of *John Lilly, so far...*

Songs of Ecstasy
This art booklet published to commemorate Carolyn Mary Kleefeld's opening exhibit of visionary paintings and poems at the Gallerie Illuminati in Santa Monica, CA in 1990, includes prose, nine color photographs of paintings and nine poems.

Mavericks of the Mind: Conversations for the New Millennium
by David Jay Brown and Rebecca McClen Novick
Carolyn Mary Kleefeld is interviewed, along with other leading-edge thinkers such as Allen Ginsberg, Timothy Leary, Rupert Sheldrake and John Lilly.
"This collection serves as a manual for expanding consciousness, dissolving archaic belief systems, and preparing us for the challenges of the new millennium."
— Crossing Press

FORTHCOMING BOOKS *by the* AUTHOR:

Pagan Love Poems for Living and Dying
A collection of poetry written over the last ten years

Indian Love Songs
Poetic odes to the Beloved written in collaboration with David Wayne Dunn

For fine art cards and information on Carolyn Mary Kleefeld's art, appearances and forthcoming books, contact Atoms Mirror Atoms, Inc., P.O. Box 221693, Carmel, CA 93922 Phone (831) 626-2924, or browse the website at http://elfi.com/illuminati.html

To order Carolyn Mary Kleefeld's books or for additional information, contact Merrill-West Publishing, P.O. Box 1227, Carmel, CA 93921 e-mail: info@voyagertarot.com Phone (831) 644-9096, or browse the website at http://www.voyagertarot.com

READER'S NOTES

READER'S NOTES